UDL AT SCALE

TEACHING, ENGAGING, AND THRIVING IN HIGHER ED

James M. Lang and Michelle D. Miller, SERIES EDITORS

UDL AT SCALE

Whole-Campus Universal Design for Learning

THOMAS J. TOBIN

University of Oklahoma Press : Norman

Publication of this book is made possible through the generosity of Edith Kinney Gaylord.

The author declares that he has not used any type of generative artificial intelligence tools for the writing of this book, nor for the creation of images, graphics, tables, or their corresponding captions.

UDL at Scale: Whole-Campus Universal Design for Learning is Volume 9 in the Teaching, Engaging, and Thriving in Higher Ed series.

Library of Congress Cataloging-in-Publication Data

Names: Tobin, Thomas J. author
Title: UDL at scale : whole-campus universal design for learning / Thomas J. Tobin.
Description: Norman : University of Oklahoma Press, 2026. | Series: Teaching, engaging, and thriving in higher ed ; Volume 9 | Includes bibliographical references and index. | Summary: "A highly anticipated follow-up volume from a leading voice on Universal Design for Learning (UDL) in the classroom" – Provided by the publisher. Provided by publisher.
Identifiers: LCCN 2025045074 | ISBN 9780806197050 hardcover | ISBN 978-0-8061-9706-7 (paperback)
Subjects: LCSH: Inclusive education | Instructional systems–Design | Education, Higher–Aims and objectives | Individualized instruction
Classification: LCC LC1200 .T64 2026
LC record available at https://lccn.loc.gov/2025045074

The paper in this book meets the guidelines for permanence and durability of the Committee on Production Guidelines for Book Longevity of the Council on Library Resources, Inc. ∞

The manufacturer's authorized representative in the EU for product safety is Mare Nostrum Group B.V., Mauritskade 21D, 1091 GC Amsterdam, The Netherlands, email: gpsr@mare-nostrum.co.uk.

Perfection is achieved, not when there is nothing more to add, but when there is nothing left to take away.

—Antoine de Saint-Exupéry, *Airman's Odyssey*

CONTENTS

ACKNOWLEDGMENTS

This book is the fruit of many years of conversations, experimentation, research, and hard work on the part of scholars, designers, instructors, and administrators around the world. I have been privileged to learn with and from colleagues who have created new ways to frame universal design for learning (UDL), taking it far beyond its roots in disability-support work for teachers in elementary and secondary schools. I am deeply grateful to the researchers, scholars, designers, and instructors who have shared their struggles, insights, and paths with me, through interviews, collaborations, writing, or hiring me as a consultant to help them scale up their colleges' and universities' UDL efforts. You'll encounter many of these people's stories and work in this book, and many more have brought key questions and ideas into the larger conversation around where we all should go next with UDL. My deep gratitude and thanks go to my colleagues in the United States, Canada, Hungary, Ireland, the United Kingdom, Australia, South Africa, Iceland, Germany, the Philippines, Portugal, France, Italy, Saudi Arabia, Colombia, and Trinidad and Tobago:

Judy Ableser, Ahmed Al-Azawei, Huda Ali, H. Samy Alim, Noah Arney, Heather Avery, Emiliano Ayala, Susan Baglieri, Haboun Bair, John Baker, Lauren Barbeau, Constanza Bartholomae, Jamie D. Basham, Adria Battaglia, Param Bedi, Kirsten Behling, Trina Bianchini, Georgieann Bogdan, Susan Bowen, Roy Bowery, Séan Bracken, Nicole Brewer, Brian R. Bryant, Sheri Burgstahler, Jordan

Cameron, Ben Campbell (the Australian one), Ben Campbell (the North Carolina one), Christy Campbell, Matthew Capp, Sarah Rose Cavanagh, Carolee Cline, Karen Ray Costa, Susan Cullen, Therese Cumming, Rachel Currie-Rubin, sarah madoka currie, Barry Dahl, Toni D'Angelo, Patricia L. Davies, Erin DeSilva, Loren Duffy, Patti Dyjur, Dave Edyburn, Anya S. Evmenova, Frederic Fovet, John Fritz, Andratesha Fritzgerald, Anna Greene, Jeffrey A. Greene, Christine Grima-Farrell, Richard Hall, Danielle Hamblin, Carrie Hansel, Maureen Haran, Jina Hardy, Madelyn Hart, Ann Heelan, Katrina Herold, Elizabeth Hitches, Aleksandra Hollingshead, Joe Houghton, Leonia Houston, Sarah Humphreys, Shawn Iles, Mark Jenkins, Anita Jones, Sam C. Johnston, Cait Kirby, Darla Kearney, Ranya Khan, Margaret E. King-Sears, Kjetil A. Knarlag, Megan Kohler, Thaddeus Langostine, Karsten Lundqvist, Helen La, Helen Lee, Gloria Ladson-Billings, Randy Laist, Diana LaRocco, Julia Remsik Larsen, Rob LeGary, Carolyn Lightfoot, Katie Linder, Sam Matychuk, Darlene McLennan, Kevin Merry, Christine Moskell, Loui Lord Nelson, Tolu Noah, Liz Norell, Michelle Ockers, Elinor Jeanette Olaussen, Ashley Olsen, Min Wook Ok, Lindsay Sanborn Owen, Django Paris, Patrick Parslow, Luis Perez, Chavella Pittman, Niamh Plunkett, Marcus Popetz, Allison Posey, Katie Rose Guest Pryal, Jennifer Pusateri, Mary Quirke, Patti Ralabate, Anna Redstone, Alexandra Rockey, Kristan Rodriguez, David H. Rose, Megan C. Rose, Marvin Roski, Dara Ryder, Melissa Sanjeh, Catherine Schelly, Carl Schottmiller, Fabio Serenelli, Kyle Shachmut, Dana Sheehan, Sarah E. Silverman, Chemène Sinson, Amy Sjoberg, Frances G. Smith, David Smulders, Craig Spooner, Abraham Stefanidis, Morgan Strimel, Seanna Takacs, Ruth Templeton, Jess Thompson, Marc Thompson, Grace Troupe, Lynn Truong, Nicole Tucker-Smith, Joseph M. Valente, George Van Horn, Malte Walkowiak, Brian Wojcik, Sonya Woods, Mary C. Wright, Tim Wrye, Justin Wylie, Shira Yalon-Chamowitz, Jeffrey Yan, Alfred Matthew Yankovic, Junsong Zhang, and Ling Zhang.

I extend gratitude and thanks as well to my friends at CAST, the organization where UDL was first framed, and whose stewardship has seen the UDL framework through three major updates. I owe a special thanks to Andrew Berzanskis, Derek Krissoff, and Michelle Miller for their editorial support as I was writing the manuscript for this book, as well as to Lillian Nave and Kavita Rao for their insightful feedback as early readers—all of your ideas have made this a stronger, more practical book. I'm also deeply grateful to my partner Mary Ann Tobin, for her constant support and deep commitment to equity and access. She's a UDL rock star in her own right (look her up, y'all)!

I am proud to introduce you in these pages to many people and their organizations, without whom I could not have written this book. Any errors or infelicities that you may find herein are entirely my own. In my research and writing process, I have relied on and connected with many more people than can fit into an acknowledgements list, so to everyone who is doing the hard and necessary work of lowering access barriers for our learners—and for ourselves—this book is for you . . . and for your boss!

INTRODUCTION

What is the most pressing concern on the minds of college and university deans, provosts, presidents, chancellors, rectors, and board members?

Most of us answer this question with "our students." It's right there in our mission, vision, and value statements. Across all sorts of higher education—from further education, technical, and community colleges to selective private four-year institutions, open-enrollment regional public universities, and research-focused flagship institutions—one thing we all have in common is a dedication to providing our learners with quality learning experiences that will support them as they move on to their next steps in life. We use this kind of aspirational and motivational language at key moments in students' experiences with us: when they first become part of our communities, as they move from year to year within our programs of study, and when we confer their credentials at graduation.

Practically speaking, though, as institutional leaders at all levels, we spend the majority of our time and energy supporting student learning indirectly—the everyday answer to "our most pressing concern" is, bluntly, "the budget." Keeping our institutions running is a daunting task. We are responsible for finding new students; serving current students, instructors, and staff members; and governing ourselves by ensuring that the funds coming in from tuition, state support, grants, and endowments roughly balance against the funds being spent on staff paychecks, vendor invoices, research projects, scholarships, dining halls, and fixing the roof on the science building.

The largest barrier that most of us face in running our colleges and universities is resource allocation. Where we spend our funds, where we assign people to work, and how we prioritize responsibilities—all of these are measurable markers of our collective priorities as institutions. Our financial and human resources are finite. When we think about how we spend our time, we can, and should, find ways to lower access barriers, keep students and employees with us for longer, and streamline our systems and processes in ways that honor our mission, vision, and value statements. That's what this book is all about.

Across all sorts of institutions practitioners are experiencing a common set of challenges: our learners come to us from an increasingly wide variety of circumstances, levels of preparation, economic capacities, and ability profiles.

That's good news. More people are able to engage in higher education than ever before, including learners whom we would not have accepted or been able to support even ten or twenty years ago. It also creates challenges for us. We are collectively familiar with the individual-accommodation model for responding to learners whose needs fall outside some mythical "average": we make one change, one time, for one person at a time. This model stretches—and often breaks—when it's not just one or two learners anymore, but 30 to 50 percent of our learners asking for "one change, one time, for one person." We are collectively waking up to recognize that, as I overheard two CIOs talking with each other at a recent EDUCAUSE conference, "it's not 2 percent of our students anymore (if it ever was). It's more like 40 percent of students—and faculty, too. We've got to have flexible systems or we're going to drown in work" (personal communication, October 11, 2023).

The huge demand for accommodations is cracking our existing support systems. It's so important that EDUCAUSE itself recommends "providing universal access to institutional services" (EDUCAUSE 2023) as a key shift everyone in higher education must enact to continue our institutional resilience. And because accommodations aren't a sustainable response to the variability among learners once we reach a certain scale, we're now faced with a related challenge. How can we reduce the need for individual accommodations through the everyday work of our entire institutions? *UDL at Scale* is a how-to guide for doing exactly that.

Welcome to this How-To Guide

I've spent the last 30-plus years in just about every seat there is in higher education: undergraduate and graduate student, instructor, designer, system administrator, educational developer, conference director, unit leader. Throughout all of those experiences, my work has focused on how to lower access barriers for everyone involved in our work: learners, instructors, support staff, administrators, and the communities whom we serve and in which we operate. Since I started in the mid-1990s, we have collectively accomplished a lot in terms of making higher education more accessible, welcoming people whom we previously excluded in many ways. Over that time, I've studied, written about, and shared practical ways in which we can put our goals of providing access to higher education into practice.

When Kirsten Behling and I wrote *Reach Everyone, Teach Everyone: Universal Design for Learning in Higher Education* in 2018, our aim was to introduce the UDL framework to an audience of educators who largely had not yet heard about the approach.

I've now worked with dozens of vocational-education, further-ed, community-college, four-year, and university partners across the world to introduce them to UDL and help them to improve their persistence, retention, and student-satisfaction metrics—including fifteen institutions that have made the commitment to UDL across their entire operations. You'll hear some of their stories as you read this book.

Today, UDL is gaining wider recognition in higher education, and it's time for us to move collectively beyond the efforts of individual designers and instructors and take advantage of the power of "access at scale," going beyond just making materials accessible because the law says we have to do so. As we are looking to attract new learners, keep our existing learners with us, and support our institutional reputations in our communities, adopting the UDL framework allows us to bring access into our core work and identity—to make access "just how we do thing here."

Welcome, Readers. Give this Book to Others!

This is a book for busy administrators and campus leaders that offers an executive-focus understanding of the background, research, and action steps for framing, testing, and adopting the UDL framework at a systemic level at your institution. Throughout the book, you'll encounter real stories of campus leaders at all levels who have identified ways to use UDL broadly to address enrollment, persistence, and retention concerns—and along the way lower barriers for students, instructors, and staff members.

Whether you are a campus leader with a formal title or you are a thought leader who wants to help move beyond individual efforts at lowering access barriers for learners, this book will guide your work as you define the challenges you want to address, build your team of UDL champions, create compelling messaging for your campus community, map your goals and measurements for your UDL-at-scale project, and assess the work and creativity that your colleagues put into becoming a UDL institution.

This book is also something of a "secret boss training" vehicle, as well. UDL is a topic that many of us with established careers never had the opportunity to learn about in our formal studies or professional-development work. This tends to be more common the higher up we go in the leadership hierarchies of our colleges and universities: operations-level supervisors largely know about UDL, but our colleagues in the C-suite are often less familiar with the model. Systemic changes happen with support from campus leadership as well as commitment from everyone who oversees and does the hard work. So, please, read this book and then *lend it to your boss.*

Instructional Structures and the Learning Institution

In return for our investment of time, funding, and resources, what benefits do our colleges and universities get from adopting UDL principles in the design of our interactions? As you will experience in the chapters of this book, the reward is three-fold: (1) a smoother, more successful experience for our learners; (2) a culture of support and collaborative effort; and (3) improved learner persistence, retention, and satisfaction.

Over the years, we've had a robust conversation about why accessibility is a noble goal for colleges and universities (Ableser and Moore 2018). Despite our common challenges of fragmented service silos, unclear compliance definitions, limited human and financial resources, and lack of guidance from campus leadership beyond meeting legal mandates, we would be hard pressed to find anyone who doesn't think that making content and interactions accessible to the broadest possible audience is the right thing to do.

We would also be hard pressed to find many people who are expert in exactly how to make basic accessibility—or even what we might call "mere access"—a reality across campus. Sure, we have laws in place, as well as industry standards, working groups, and advocacy efforts. But still, at the end of the day, we also have lawsuits, and our dark secret is that almost none of us feels, deep down, that our institutions are yet fully compliant with even the basic legal requirements, let alone ready to say publicly that we are accessible institutions.

Campus leaders seem—almost uniformly—to think about instructors and course offerings when we think about accessibility and inclusive design (Borghans and Golsteyn 2015): how can instructors make their courses more accessible? When presidents and provosts think of other access barriers, they invariably add their institutions' websites in terms of video captioning and image alt-text tagging (Brown 2018). This low-hanging fruit encompasses only the maintenance tasks performed by the most potentially powerful accessibility players on campus: the staff.

Information technology (IT), library, and academic-support units are in the best position to influence how all of our college and university constituents experience systems, processes, content, and tools (Burgstahler and Vinten-Johansen 2017). We should adopt UDL as we design interfaces, procure and purchase staff tools, and support inclusive-design initiatives on our campuses (Bowery and Houston 2017). We have great language to use in conversations about accessibility (Moriarty 2018), lofty goals about providing access to education for everyone (Thompson, Jenkins and Campbell 2018), and strategy-level milestones to target. But how do we actually do it?

The institutions that are furthest along in their accessibility efforts tend to have service-unit leaders who share certain practices. They typically chop off the end of the word "accessibility," focusing their efforts on expanding *access*, regardless of the ability profiles of their learners. They shift their goals away from just making content accessible and look instead at making interactions easier to engage in (Cullen 2018). And they have largely moved beyond the mental model of universal design (UD) in the physical environment, which is static, bounded, and predictable—instead designing interactions according to UDL, which sees interactions as dynamic, open, and emergent (DeSilva, Nemeroff and Lopez 2017).

That's all advanced-level accessibility, though. What most of us are after are starting points.

The Origins of UDL

When it was founded in 1984, CAST used to stand for the Center for Applied Specialized Technology, but these days they have dropped the words all together and just go by the acronym CAST. The researchers who started this non-profit company, led by David Rose and Ann Meyer, initially had a goal to "revolutionize the way that students with special needs were taught by introducing technology that would allow teachers and students to customize their learning experiences" (Thibodeau 2021).

In the mid-1990s, the researchers at CAST shared the foundational model of UDL: when humans learn things, we have to active three different chemical pathways in our brains, each of which corresponds roughly to a phase of the learning process. They also saw from experiments with learners that having more than one way to engage in each of the three general phases of learning (engagement, content, and practice) increased the chances that learning will happen, stick, and be available for later retrieval and practice. The three UDL principles simplify a messy and complex learning process into a repeatable but flexible set of ways to approach the design of learning experiences. Figure 0.1 shows the "brain networks" diagram of the three UDL principles: design multiple means of engagement, representation, and action & expression.

Universal Design for Learning

Affective networks:
THE WHY OF LEARNING

How learners get engaged and stay motivated. How they are challenged, excited, or interested. These are affective dimensions.

Stimulate interest and motivation for learning

Recognition networks:
THE WHAT OF LEARNING

How we gather facts and categorize what we see, hear, and read. Identifying letters, words, or an author's style are recognition tasks.

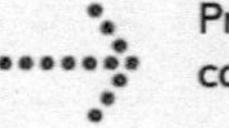

Present information and content in different ways

Strategic networks:
THE HOW OF LEARNING

Planning and performing tasks. How we organize and express our ideas. Writing an essay or solving a math problem are strategic tasks

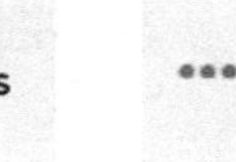

Differentiate the ways that students can express what they know

FIGURE. 0.1: The UDL "Brain Networks" Diagram. © CAST, used with permission.

Figure 0.1 shows the affective, recognition, and strategic networks in the brain, represented by darker shading in three simplified brain diagrams. The idea to take away from the "three brains" diagram is that while learning doesn't follow the same methods, structures, or approaches (indeed, every learning situation is a unique combination of factors), the learning process itself is broadly consistent, and we can design learning experiences to strengthen each of the three phases: getting and staying engaged, taking in information, and practicing with new concepts and ideas.

As the researchers in CAST recruited elementary special-education teachers to experiment with and develop the UDL framework (you'll learn more about it in chapter 1), they recognized that many of the barriers that learners encountered weren't because of something "wrong" with the learners but rather because their environments weren't designed to support them well. This contrasts the medical model of disability, in which we perceive people themselves as broken, diseased, or undeveloped (see White, Ollendick and Bray 2011), with the social model of disability, in which we accept that people are remarkably variable, and that barriers exist not in their bodies or identities, but rather in the environments around them. People who use wheelchairs to get around are not disabled because of their bodies, but because the built environment doesn't always take them into account: the universal design features of curb cuts and ramps are outcomes of the social model.

The goal for CAST evolved from supporting individual learners with assistive technology eventually to focus on the "disabilities of schools" instead of the "disabilities of the individual." So, even in their earliest days of working in the special-education arena in elementary schools, the researchers at CAST understood that individual teacher efforts in classrooms aren't sufficient to address gaps, barriers, and exclusionary practices. It's an irony, then, that the majority of UDL implementations in colleges and universities today are at the individual-practitioner level—thanks largely to one-off efforts from the practitioners who have the time, resources, privilege, and interest in doing the work of barrier-lowering around access. Paradoxically, one reason why UDL hasn't yet gotten traction at scale in higher education is its very flexibility.

The Plus-One Approach

Rather than starting with CAST's neuroscience-based three brain networks and multiple means of engagement, representation, and action & expression, a more manageable starting point is "plus one" thinking, an approach I first shared in *Reach Everyone, Teach Everyone* (Tobin 2018). Briefly, think of the interactions that your instructors and student-support units offer to people, and think of how they might interact in just one more way than happens now. Think of how learners interact and engage with

- **content.** This is where most of us start when we think about lowering access barriers. Make a transcript or captions for videos on your website. Create a quick explainer video to accompany written directions about how to select and apply for courses in future semesters.
- **each other.** As learners study together, find help from peers, and connect for social support, design more than one way that they can communicate, such as email discussion groups, in-person meetups around topics or issues, and online collaboration spaces that provide chat, whiteboards, and other study-together tools.
- **their instructors.** Learners shouldn't have to dig out the syllabus to know how best to connect with their

instructors. Ask instructors to communicate multiple ways for learners to connect, both in groups and one-to-one. Hold office hours in person at the campus food court as well as online via Zoom or another video-chat tool. Offer feedback check-ins via email or phone call.

- **support staff.** Librarians are way ahead of most of us, here. They offer multiple ways to connect with them: text chat, phone calls, in-person consultations, video-chat tools. Ask your colleagues in academic counseling, mental-health counseling, information technology (IT), and other service areas to do similar expansions of ways learners can take advantage of their services.

UDL dovetails with and supports our current expansion, outreach, and retention efforts by asking us to think about learning interactions in an especially broad sense. Wherever learners encounter new systems, processes, information, people, and ideas, we can make their experience smoother by acknowledging and designing for the variability they bring to those circumstances in as many facets of our work as possible.

Consistent and Systematic

Running throughout this book is a theme of "in every instance." In the 1960s and 1970s, architect Ron Mace coined the term "universal design," or UD, to describe a way of recognizing and systematically addressing inaccessible conditions in the built environment. As a wheelchair user, Mace encountered barriers in buildings, such as stairs leading to entrance doors, where individual responses—reforming the built environment by request, one piece at a time—would be inadequate, cumbersome, inconsistent, or impossible. Mace's work and advocacy spawned an entirely new way of thinking about how humans, with all of their variability in physical attributes, interact with the world around them, identifying and addressing disabling conditions in the environment, rather than finding fault with the humans who use such spaces.

The initial framework of UD has led to a well-defined universe of standards, minimum conditions, and repeatable practices that should be implemented *in every instance* across the built environment to ensure a common level of physical access to buildings and designed spaces. A large part of the reasons that UD standards are enshrined in both laws and architecture-and-building-industry practices today is their broad applicability to varying spaces and use cases. UD standards do not attempt to remove, anticipate, or remedy all possible barriers—just the big, obvious, measurable ones.

By establishing a minimum width for doorways, or mandating ramps, lifts, or elevators where stairs are also present, we can measure successful UD implementations concretely *in every instance*, and we can determine clearly whether given designs meet UD criteria. For instance, escalators are somewhat more accessible than staircases, but escalators still fall short of the access-for-most goals of universal design.

Like UD, universal design for learning (UDL) began as a series of observations about how individual supports and affordances for learners could be addressed systematically and proactively in the design of learning interactions. Wherever learners interact with materials, one another, instructors, support staff members, their institutions, and their communities, UDL proposes that we can lower access barriers by providing multiple means of engagement, representation, and action & expression for learners engaged in those learning interactions.

In the built environment, all doors can be described in ways that either meet or fail the UD criteria. In learning interactions, we're not describing doors or ramps, but engagements themselves, as designed for the variability among potential learners. And learners have a nearly infinite variety of characteristics and ways of engaging with the content and people involved in learning interactions. Learner variability is a keystone element of the UDL framework. Indeed, learner variability is the reason an approach like UDL is needed in the first place. We assume that learners will come into learning interactions from highly variable perspectives, so we design our interactions to contain multiple means for the elements of the learning process to take place, in the hopes that we are lowering barriers for as wide a swath of learners as possible.

The flexibility of UDL is part of the framework itself: the model relies on only a few fixed principles and asks practitioners to apply those principles in multivariate ways. This is in contrast to the large number of fixed principles in UD, where practitioners can clearly understand whether UD principles are being implemented well *in every instance*. This raises a fundamental question for practitioners of UDL in higher education. What are the measurable, comparable, and consistent markers of UDL done well that we can apply *in every instance* in order to be able to move beyond individual learning interactions and create, apply, and assess UDL in its broadest applications?

Scaling Up with UDL

When we think about UDL at scale—across entire programs, departments, schools, colleges, and universities—what we're after is the sort of consistency in the application of the three principles, nine guidelines, and thirty-six considerations of the UDL framework that has allowed for universal design (UD) to have become encoded so strongly in the architectural world. What does UDL look like *in every instance*, and how can we clearly determine whether given implementations satisfy the demands of the model? An examination of the component descriptors in the phrase "universal design for learning" offers a way to define and delimit our UDL-at-scale task.

Our UDL-at-scale criteria or standards must first be universal. In UD, practitioners have a bounded, finite set of standards to guide designs for the built environment, based on the ways in which physical bodies move through and interact with such spaces. UDL at scale similarly must consider a set of bounded, finite actions that we take *in every instance,* based on the ways in which our physical and mental selves engage in learning interactions.

UDL-at-scale criteria must also focus on the design of learning interactions; that is, engagements that are preplanned for learner variability (but not necessarily preprogrammed—more on this distinction later). In UD, the built environment is intentionally structured for multiple users and access cases, based on both practical experience and theory-based constraints. The power of UD, as a theoretical construct, is its ability to encounter novel physical spaces and predict, plan, and purpose them for multifunctional uses. UDL is also concerned with lowering access barriers. At scale, we need a set of design principles that are applied in every instance, and that can be used to predict and plan access expansions among learning interactions across the range of campus services.

At scale, UDL must limit itself to a bounding factor. The bounding factor in UD is space. How do humans most accessibly make use of the built environment? In UDL at scale, the bounding factor is learning. Regardless of who drives, guides, facilitates, or teaches, UDL at scale aims to increase access to—and the effectiveness of—interactions that learners have with materials, one another, professionals, and communities.

More Effective, More Efficient

A fruitful way to define UDL at scale is to find comparable knowledge domains where there are already assessment and measurement standards. For instance, we already have measurable and consistent criteria for the effectiveness of the design of learning interactions in classroom and lab settings (see the work of Kirkpatrick and several other Scholarship of Teaching and Learning, or SoTL, scholars). Applying similar criteria to UDL at scale allows us truly to measure the impact of our UDL implementations in a consistent and comparable fashion, all while preserving the flexibility that is a hallmark of the UDL framework. Colleagues in the psychological sciences, especially, have been calling for greater rigor in the definition and testing of the UDL model. The approach in this book offers such a path for rigor, at scale.

The UDL framework has been shown to lower barriers and increase learner persistence, retention, and satisfaction in individual K–12, college, and university classrooms. Recent large-scale studies demonstrate that learners who have a sense of voice, choice, agency, safety, and belonging in their overall programs of study are significantly more likely to complete their educational goals successfully (see Tobin 2018).

Further, inclusive design practices like UDL are most effective when adopted broadly, at the systemic level. Much of the current literature about UDL focuses on steps that individual instructors and designers can take. The field of campus-wide and systemic UDL application is relatively young. Theorists and practitioners are creating new approaches to help colleges and universities to discover the most needed places in their services and offerings where lowered barriers will have the greatest initial impact (cf. Cameron 2016, Tobin and Behling 2018, Nave 2019 and Herold 2022).

This book is intended to provide campus leaders with practical approaches for system-wide adoption of inclusive-design practices, using data and evidence from recent large-scale studies (such as Manly 2022). Using data from campus-wide UDL adoption efforts, as well as proven project-management, change-management, and leadership-vision techniques and tools, this book supports practitioners and leaders who wish to spearhead wider efforts to lower access barriers for learners across their institutions through the establishment of new institutional, cultural, practical, and policy-based structures.

What a Long, Strange Trip It's Been

The processes you will encounter in this book typically take years to initiate, plan, execute, monitor, close, and operationalize. While I will share the ideas and strategies in this book in a sequence, there is considerable overlap among the various elements and phases of any UDL scaling-up effort. Wherever possible, I provide estimates in terms of time, human effort, and resources needed for completion—along with stories from people who have actually done the things successfully. As you think about implementing your own scale-up projects at your institutions, be prepared to invest significant time and resources into your work. There's no escaping the reality that addressing access barriers takes intentional time and effort. Fortunately, our return on this investment pays us back many times over in increased learner persistence, retention, and satisfaction.

How to Use This Book

UDL at Scale is intended to be a how-to manual for adopting UDL and related inclusive-design techniques at the level of an entire college, university, or institution. Along the way, you will encounter case narratives from colleges and universities that are at various points in their UDL journeys. You'll find good practices, advice from experienced professionals, and ways to assess and measure the impact of your efforts. The information contained in this book is presented as a process, keyed to critical milestones and cultural patterns that make the actual adoption of a campus-wide change easier and smoother.

In chapter 1, we start with a few definitions, some history, and the business case for why UDL is a bottom-line budget approach that helps to increase student persistence, retention, and satisfaction: key drivers for institutional continuation. Chapter 2 contains ideas, peer cases, and evidence to share with your campus colleagues as you make the argument for lowering access barriers as an institutional priority. In chapter 3, we build into a conversation about how to create conditions that make at-scale UDL possible: frame the cultural argument for UDL adoption alongside the infrastructure requirements that allow that cultural change to proceed well. In chapter 4, we'll explore how to signal that UDL is permitted, via the establishment of policy and practices that set the agenda, tone, and parameters for effective changes and sustained cultural shifts.

To make UDL a supported part of your organizational culture, chapter 5 shares the specifics of actually doing campus-wide UDL implementations, with examples from institutional leaders who have successfully adopted UDL across their instruction and service-point operations. Chapter 6 deals with how to reward UDL work and evolve campus culture using the levers of funding, prestige, exclusivity, and incentive. In chapter 7, we will talk about what happens after we get to scale to make UDL an expected part of your institution's identity and work. What does becoming a UDL institution allow you now to do in terms of your curricula and planning? The book ends with a conclusion that is different from the messaging around UDL that is common today. Instead of a social-justice argument (that UDL is a way to address deep inequities among various elements of our society), I'll argue that when we apply UDL across all of the service touchpoints of our institutions, it is a sound business decision: we keep more

TABLE 0.1

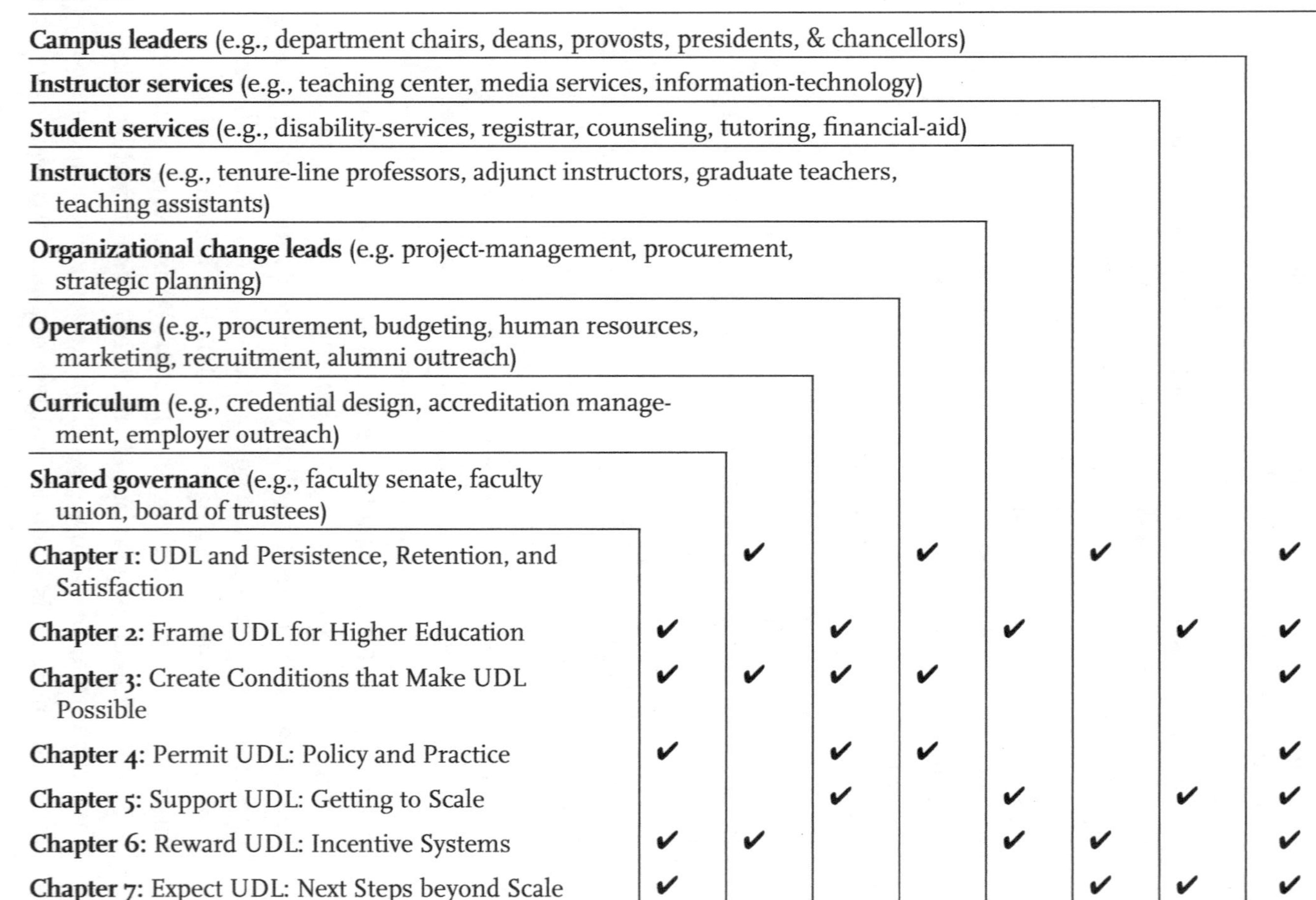

	Shared governance (e.g., faculty senate, faculty union, board of trustees)	Curriculum (e.g., credential design, accreditation management, employer outreach)	Operations (e.g., procurement, budgeting, human resources, marketing, recruitment, alumni outreach)	Organizational change leads (e.g. project-management, procurement, strategic planning)	Instructors (e.g., tenure-line professors, adjunct instructors, graduate teachers, teaching assistants)	Student services (e.g., disability-services, registrar, counseling, tutoring, financial-aid)	Instructor services (e.g., teaching center, media services, information-technology)	Campus leaders (e.g., department chairs, deans, provosts, presidents, & chancellors)
Chapter 1: UDL and Persistence, Retention, and Satisfaction		✔		✔		✔		✔
Chapter 2: Frame UDL for Higher Education	✔		✔		✔		✔	✔
Chapter 3: Create Conditions that Make UDL Possible	✔	✔	✔	✔				✔
Chapter 4: Permit UDL: Policy and Practice	✔		✔	✔				✔
Chapter 5: Support UDL: Getting to Scale			✔		✔		✔	✔
Chapter 6: Reward UDL: Incentive Systems	✔	✔			✔	✔		✔
Chapter 7: Expect UDL: Next Steps beyond Scale	✔					✔	✔	✔

learners with us as they work toward their goals, and we increase the strength, financial health, and reputation of our colleges and universities.

UDL is all about offering people optimized choices in how they move through the interactions that we design for them, and this book is no different. Although I hope that the entire book will be useful for every reader, I have created Table 0.1 as a suggested first-read chart, depending on your role on campus or the goal of your campus-change initiatives. Chapters marked with a check mark are read-first recommendations.

A Call to Action

As you begin thinking about UDL at scale in your college, university, or institution, take two actions to help you get the most out of your experience of this book. First, select a path to follow. Whether you experience the ideas in the book in a linear way or you shift from one element of the scaling-up process to another based on your role or needs, keep that clear goal in mind and compare the examples and practices in this book to the situation in your own organization. Second, think of the amount of effort, time, funding, and resources your organization already invests in its core-mission activities: research, curriculum, teaching, marketing, learner support, alumni relations, and so on. As you encounter the ideas in this book, think of how you can frame UDL to your peers as a similarly mission-critical effort, one that helps with bottom-line concerns like persistence, retention, and satisfaction.

The Requisite Disclaimer

In this book, I talk about a number of global laws related to accessibility, inclusive design, and UDL. The information contained in this book is provided for educational purposes only, is not a substitute for legal advice, and should not be construed as the rendering of legal opinions. While I am not a lawyer, the ideas and materials herein are based on more than thirty years of practice and collaboration with legal scholars, campus leaders, educators, educational developers, disability-services advocates, and accessibility professionals. With that, let's dive in to what UDL does for a campus when it is implemented and adopted at scale: we'll "start with the 'why,'" as our UDL colleague Eric Moore advocates (Nave 2018). We'll examine how to make UDL possible, permitted, supported, rewarded, and—finally—expected.

1

UDL AND PERSISTENCE, RETENTION, AND SATISFACTION

In this chapter, we'll set the stage for universal design for learning (UDL) at scale. You'll discover more about what UDL is, where it comes from, how it got started in higher education, how we might use it as an umbrella approach to a number of efforts to broaden access to higher education, and why UDL is a sound business decision.

The Basics of UDL

UDL has its roots in disability-support work with K–12 learners. David Rose and his colleagues at what was then known as the Center for Applied Special Technology (today they go by just their acronym, CAST) argue that UDL "puts the tag 'disabled' where it belongs—on the curriculum, not the learner. The curriculum is disabled when it does not meet the needs of diverse learners" (Council for Exceptional Children 2011). In the 1990s, CAST compared the academic success rates among diverse groups of students in US public elementary and secondary schools. Was it an indication of students' ability when some seemed unable to pay attention to their teachers after fifteen minutes of lecturing? Were students whose first language was not English being punished unfairly because they couldn't take notes fast enough? Why were students who did not have access to computers weaker than their peers on writing concepts?

CAST looked holistically at student demographics, methods of instruction, and curriculum design, initially seeking a frame that would fit all these differences into one instructional method. Their finding, however, was that variability is the norm: no two students learn alike, regardless of ability. Curriculum design at the time was largely monolithic, forcing all students to receive information and demonstrate skills in only one way. David Gordon writes about the need to recognize and design for learner variability:

> Options are essential to learning, because no single way of presenting information, no single way of responding to information, and no single way of engaging students will work across the diversity of students [who] populate our classrooms. Alternatives reduce barriers to learning for students with disabilities while enhancing learning opportunities for everyone. (Council for Exceptional Children 2011)

CAST began to frame a design approach that anticipated the variability learners brought to the interactions in elementary and secondary education systems. Their resulting framework is called Universal Design for Learning (UDL), which is contained in three principles specific to learning and neurological processing, focused on three brain-based information networks, as you encountered in the introduction to this book. Table 1.1 reproduces the earliest expression of UDL.

It is important to note that, in the UDL framework, there is no requirement for information to be presented in all of its different

TABLE 1.1 The Earliest UDL Guidelines, 1999–2009. (CAST, 2008)

Brain Network	*Question*	*Solution*
Recognition	The "what" of learning. How do we gather information?	Present information in multiple ways.
Strategic	The "how" of learning. How do we express our ideas?	Differentiate the ways that students can express what they know.
Affective	The "why" of learning. How do we motivate learners?	Find a way to connect with student interests. Provide multiple methods of engaging with the material.

possible permutations, or in one unique way per student. Rather, UDL posits that designing for learner variability ahead of time—before instructors even know their students yet—is the most effective way to reduce individual-accommodation needs. In other words, offering students optimized choices in how to recognize, engage with, and report back the information they learned increases the chances that instructors can connect with their students and their learning needs.

Today, the UDL Guidelines are at version 3.0. Each of the three principles is supported by nine guidelines, which are further broken down into thirty-six considerations—each supported by research and evidence. While this book is not intended to be a detailed dive into the UDL guidelines (indeed, doing so can be counterproductive in scaling-up efforts), it is useful to know the structure and basic content of the UDL guidelines. This chart in figure 1.1 is reproduced from the CAST website; readers who are curious about learning the details of the UDL guidelines should visit udlguidelines.cast.org.

	Design Multiple Means of **Engagement**	Design Multiple Means of **Representation** 	Design Multiple Means of **Action & Expression** 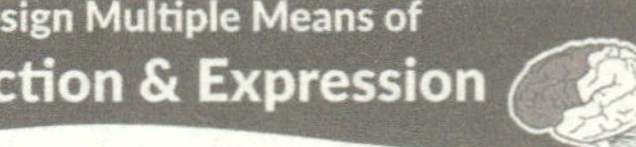
Access	Design Options for **Welcoming Interests & Identities** (7) • Optimize choice and autonomy (7.1) • Optimize relevance, value, and authenticity (7.2) • Nurture joy and play (7.3) • Address biases, threats, and distractions (7.4)	Design Options for **Perception** (1) • Support opportunities to customize the display of information (1.1) • Support multiple ways to perceive information (1.2) • Represent a diversity of perspectives and identities in authentic ways (1.3)	Design Options for **Interaction** (4) • Vary and honor the methods for response, navigation, and movement (4.1) • Optimize access to accessible materials and assistive and accessible technologies and tools (4.2)
Support	Design Options for **Sustaining Effort & Persistence** (8) • Clarify the meaning and purpose of goals (8.1) • Optimize challenge and support (8.2) • Foster collaboration, interdependence, and collective learning (8.3) • Foster belonging and community (8.4) • Offer action-oriented feedback (8.5)	Design Options for **Language & Symbols** (2) • Clarify vocabulary, symbols, and language structures (2.1) • Support decoding of text, mathematical notation, and symbols (2.2) • Cultivate understanding and respect across languages and dialects (2.3) • Address biases in the use of language and symbols (2.4) • Illustrate through multiple media (2.5)	Design Options for **Expression & Communication** (5) • Use multiple media for communication (5.1) • Use multiple tools for construction, composition, and creativity (5.2) • Build fluencies with graduated support for practice and performance (5.3) • Address biases related to modes of expression and communication (5.4)
Executive Function	Design Options for **Emotional Capacity** (9) • Recognize expectations, beliefs, and motivations (9.1) • Develop awareness of self and others (9.2) • Promote individual and collective reflection (9.3) • Cultivate empathy and restorative practices (9.4)	Design Options for **Building Knowledge** (3) • Connect prior knowledge to new learning (3.1) • Highlight and explore patterns, critical features, big ideas, and relationships (3.2) • Cultivate multiple ways of knowing and making meaning (3.3) • Maximize transfer and generalization (3.4)	Design Options for **Strategy Development** (6) • Set meaningful goals (6.1) • Anticipate and plan for challenges (6.2) • Organize information and resources (6.3) • Enhance capacity for monitoring progress (6.4) • Challenge exclusionary practices (6.5)

FIGURE 1.1: CAST UDL Guidelines, Version 3.0 (CAST, 2024). Modified with permission.

Universal Design for Learning's Higher Education Beginnings

Globally, higher education has not been as quick to adopt UDL as have our elementary- and secondary-education colleagues. UDL in higher education began in earnest in the early 2000s, when the Office of Postsecondary Education (OPE) in the US Department of Education created grants for colleges and universities seeking to bring the concept to higher education, in response to the technology-driven arguments in David Rose and Ann Meyer's book *Teaching Every Student in the Digital Age* (2002). The OPE saw the positive effects of inclusive-design efforts in elementary and secondary education and recognized that as students in those schools graduated and transitioned to college, they would expect the same breadth of learning opportunities as they had previously enjoyed. Many of those who applied for and received the federal grants were members of disability-services offices in colleges and universities. In the early 2000s, campus disability-services offices were most likely to be part of conversations about inclusive education and were the campus areas most likely to know about the work of CAST. They also saw UDL as a built-in service to improve the educational experiences of both the students with disabilities with whom they worked, and those who chose not to disclose disabilities or who had yet to come to their offices.

The OPE grants funded work to figure out how to bring inclusive design to college and university campuses, given the differences among elementary, secondary, and higher education. Grant-funded researchers recognized the difficulty in mandating any particular training or implementation scheme in college and university settings. For this reason, most grantees created implementation frameworks not through a disability-services lens but through diversity narratives. The goal of the OPE grants was to increase awareness about inclusive design in higher education.

CAST partnered with different OPE-grant institutions as part of this grant program.

At Temple University, the OPE-grant project included UDL in its orientations for new faculty and staff members, who were then asked to incorporate the principles in their courses and student interactions. The University of Iowa conducted a campus UDL needs assessment and developed a university-wide policy focusing on the goal of giving universal access to learning interactions. The University of Hawaii combined UDL with multiculturalism and mentoring in an effort to get campus staffers and instructors to support diverse learners better. Colorado State University's twice-funded project focused on supporting instructors by adding UDL strategies to the materials that they created for their courses. Each of these efforts was a stand-alone or pilot program. At each of the universities named, and across the grant's roster of participating institutions, attention and resources tended to focus elsewhere after the funding period.

This has been the model under which the majority of colleges and universities worldwide have approached UDL: as an evidence-based approach to design that competes with other ways of thinking and doing for scarce resources of people, funds, and time. CAST's theory that learner variability is most effectively addressed by inclusive design is supported by decades of evidence from the K–12 world. UDL is rapidly gaining recognition and adoption in higher education, but it still has not been adopted by colleges and universities to the same extent as in the K–12 realm: hence, this book.

Bringing UDL to Higher Education: Disability-Services Offices and Teaching Centers

Ideally, the combination of disability-services offices, educational developers, and interested instructors would be the trifecta that catapults UDL into wide adoption across college and university campuses. A study of disability-services providers and teaching-and-learning centers found that these two offices often do not work together on inclusive design and teaching as much as they could or should (Behling and Linder 2017). Rather, the most common collaboration between these two offices is around new-faculty orientation, in which disability-services staff members give a short overview of what they do and how they serve students. The possibility is there, but typical barriers—time and resources—work against active collaboration around agreed-upon sets of effective practices.

The most common advocates for UDL on college and university campuses today are the staff and instructors with roles in the disability-services office. UDL presentations at local and national conferences for higher-education disability-services providers date back to the early 2000s. The national average of students with disabilities seeking formal services from their higher education institutions is about 10 percent of the undergraduate population (Trammell and Hathway 2007; Blasey, Wang and Blasey 2023). But the population of students with disabilities is much larger than those with documented disability-accommodation requests. Many choose not to seek disability services, finding formal recognition to be too costly to pursue, or choose not to disclose their disability status formally.

There are a number of reasons for this pattern. Some college students are unaware of services, do not know that they must seek out services, or were never diagnosed in K–12 education and are effectively new to "disability status" and unaware that they qualify for services. Disability-services providers are well aware of these reasons and are used to seeing a flurry of new requests from students right before final exams or after learners have struggled for a semester. To disability-services providers, adopting UDL at scale allows us to provide support resources and structures to students who choose not to use specific disability-support services or who do not know they might need the disability-support office at all. A further benefit of scaling up is that UDL lowers access barriers in the classroom environment and beyond—across campus, unobtrusively, and early on in students' academic careers. If students can successfully navigate their courses without specific accommodations (where we make one change, one time, for one person), then they have a better chance of continuing on with their college studies.

Implementing UDL in the design of course and campus interactions also reduces the number of individual accommodations disability-services providers must implement. Doing so especially supports those one-person disability-services offices with few resources. For example, if instructors allowed extended time on all exams for all students, then the number of individual proctoring sessions for time accommodations could be cut dramatically.

As yet, educational development offices and teaching-and-learning centers have also had limited success in bringing UDL to higher education. With the mission of supporting instructors in their efforts to improve their teaching as a whole, the hundreds of centers for teaching and learning (CTLs) at colleges and universities across the globe are well placed to advocate for UDL as an inclusive-design framework. However, CTLs often have limited power to ask (or compel) everyone in the instructor ranks to adopt specific techniques, let alone reach out to student-facing service areas.

The size of CTLs varies according to the size and resources of the institutions they are designed to serve. Recent research indicates an institutional shift over the last ten years, from a model of reallocating one instructor to dedicate part of their professional time to supporting the teaching of colleagues, to a more formalized faculty-development office model, complete with staff members and a programming budget (Wright 2023).

This demonstrates the value of varying instructional strategies to reflect the needs of an increasingly diverse student body (see Beach et al. 2016).

UDL resonates with educational-development offices because it supports instructors in their efforts to reach diverse learners. As more students are admitted to advanced studies from more varied backgrounds, levels of preparation, and ability profiles, learner variability has increased dramatically across all types of higher education. From community and technical colleges to research-focused universities and every other type of institution, our educational developers work with instructor colleagues to design interactions that increase student persistence, retention, and satisfaction—key performance indicators with which our campus leaders are intimately familiar.

UDL brings instructional concepts like Differentiated Instruction (DI), where instructors create various action pathways based on the variety of learners who are in their classrooms right now, and other inclusive practices under one umbrella framework that is fairly easy to understand and implement. Educational developers also tend to offer their services through multiple modalities such as in-person consultations, phone conversations, email exchanges, and self-paced training—a very UDL practice in itself.

To date, relatively few institutions of higher education have adopted the UDL framework as a formal structure in policy, systemic design, or broad-scale practices—even as most campus leaders have heard of UDL and support its goals of lowering access barriers and creating "individual and collective learning that is purposeful, motivated, and reflective; authentic, resourceful, and knowledgeable; strategic, creative, and liberatory" (CAST 2024a).

Next, we'll examine how the UDL framework allows us to approach common campus challenges differently than we ordinarily do within the structures of our higher-education institutions and systems. The history of UDL hints at ways we can use the UDL framework to address root causes of common challenges: enrollment, persistence, and retention gaps.

UDL Is an Umbrella

UDL is gaining traction among individual practitioners in higher education, and there is considerable interest in adopting UDL as the latest in a long series of buzzwords where our collective vision and goal statements are concerned. It sounds "right" for our colleges and universities to champion student agency, lower barriers, and broaden access to education, so we adopt, adapt, and evolve that language every five or ten years when we review our strategic plans. In higher education, we tend to suffer from what is often called "innovation fatigue," in which new approaches, theories, and practices come to the fore of our collective attention year after year. It can be difficult to predict which of these ideas are passing fads, which are additions to our existing toolkits, and which are foundational changes to how we engage in the business of teaching, learning, research, and scholarship.

UDL falls into the third category: it helps us to accomplish our stated mission by (a) allowing us to be better stewards of our resources, (b) re-focusing our campus cultures toward learning support, (c) folding our existing support and outreach efforts under an umbrella framework, and (d) providing concrete ways to measure what had previously been mostly subjectively-assessed outcomes, in ways that move us beyond mere accessibility.

A Brief History Talk

In order to explain why UDL helps us to achieve and maintain our institution-level goals, it may be useful to think about learner agency as it has developed over the history of education (see Bowen

2003). Until the eighteenth century, formal study was largely a commodity accessible only to the wealthy or well-connected. Early-life education was brief and non-compulsory, and most people had to seek out their own learning, training, and teaching opportunities, often through guild or other trade systems.

In the earliest universities, curricula were selected by the students, with instructors acting as guides and resources available to learners who chose their own paths through the systems of higher education. Timelines and paths to success were fluid; the commonality among most medieval and mid-renaissance universities was the competency-based examination that led to the conferral of the credential.

This model was upended in the nineteenth century, when the Industrial Revolution led to universal and compulsory education in subjects deemed necessary for the working classes. Higher education remained the bastion largely of the wealthy few, but its structure became more and more determined by the institution (see Tagg 2019). Vestiges of choice persisted, but within closed curricula coalesced into majors, and departments that divided higher learning into compartments focused on the provision of instruction rather than the learning demonstrated by students (with the exception of the dissertation process at the very end of the experience).

The twentieth century saw reactionary experiments to re-focus the school experience on learning gains rather than mere attendance: the Montessori "exploration" curriculum for early learners, ungrading practices in high schools to decouple learning from the ranking/sorting functions of grades, and open-curriculum models like the one pioneered at Reed College (Takahaski 1996). Attempts in higher education to shift quality measurements from teaching to learning were often met with resistance, not because of philosophical antipathy, but out of the sheer inertia built over time by the structures and processes of our post-industrial systems.

Working from the Middle

One reason why UDL has not yet seen wider adoption in higher education is that it started in K–12 education and assumes a top-down system of requirements already in place (more about this in chapter 2). UDL was just one of several competing models—including Universal Design for Instruction (UDI) and Universal Design for Education (UDE), among many others—that came out of that initial OPE grant program, all of which focused on expanding learner access and agency within existing educational structures.

What we've learned since those early days is what John Tagg calls the "instruction myth" (2019), in which our colleges and universities may express goals aligned with student learning, but we actually engage in, value, and measure practices that are aligned with the provision of instruction, not with the measurement of learning gains. Tagg's premise is intriguing. In practice, higher education revolves around instruction—easily measurable in course syllabi, credits, and enrollments. He calls for us to abandon this in favor of a model designed around the concept of learning, which is harder to define and measure than our current approaches. UDL offers us a middle way between inaction and total reinvention. Because UDL is designed around the learning process itself, it offers a path to scalability through iteration—a process of continuously addressing barriers and creating spaces for greater learner voice, choice, belonging, agency, and safety.

Scaling up our UDL efforts is not an intuitive process. In most of our organizations, there is a policy/practice gap between our expressed goals and instructors' actual actions in the classroom. Classroom instructors and designers are seldom at the table when standards and policies are being written, and there is often a loss of detail as policies make their way into practice. For example, the Quality and Qualifications Ireland (QQI) curriculum-assessment guidelines state explicitly that assessment evidence for various competencies and skills can be submitted by instructors in varying formats (QQI 2018, 10–11). This comes as a surprise to many further-education and college instructors in Ireland, who are asked by their institutions to provide only written evidence of their students' progress, and thus create activities that ask learners to create word-processed outputs.

Even with such specific guidance from accrediting bodies (there is similarly inclusive language in guidance documents from accreditors across North America, Europe, and the Asia/Pacific region), most colleges and universities continue to require text-based written evidence of skill-based compliance from learners. This is often not because of any active choice against greater flexibility in evidence for skills and knowledge; rather, campus administrators are so used to collecting certain types of information in certain ways that they select technology and reporting systems that cannot receive, catalog, compare, and apply alternatives. Our systems are, in many cases, literally not set up to handle anything but traditional text-file documents.

Working from the Top

Another obstacle toward widespread scaling up for UDL is a lack of support, definition, and clear guidance from the highest levels of our hierarchies. Our senior leaders—presidents, provosts, chancellors, governing councils, and boards of trustees—ordinarily operate at a level of abstraction apart from the day-to-day processes that keep institutions running. This can lead to "box checking" by frontline and middle-management leaders, in which policies and documentation espouse inclusive and ideal goals, while actual practice lags behind or even works counter to those stated goals. UDL's focus on expanding access supports a gap-closing process that empowers precisely those frontline and middle-management leaders on our campuses, placing authority in their hands while relying on support from the higher echelons of the institution for measurable results.

We won't change our educational institutions overnight; UDL affords us a way to talk about shifting our lens from instruction to learning, without destroying our existing systems outright. As a sector, higher education is already bound by legal requirements to make materials and processes minimally accessible, yet we continue to be sued for inaccessible websites and content. We already have a raft of policy statements about the ideal ways to approach our learners and the process of educating them, yet we continue to identify gaps between our vision statements and how we actually practice our craft. On the positive side of the ledger, many of our institutions are already engaged in proactive efforts to reach out to traditionally underserved populations of learners through diversity and inclusion programs. In areas where diversity and inclusion are legally challenged concepts, we can still talk about the rights of taxpayers to educational opportunities and expansion of citizen access to education as a public good.

The case for adopting universal design for learning at scale, then, has three elements to it. First, UDL allows us to bring our existing efforts together to broaden our reach under one umbrella framework that can guide practice in varied areas of our work. Second, UDL is shown to have a measurable impact on learner persistence, retention, and satisfaction (King-Sears et al. 2023), even when we control for other factors. Third, UDL provides a flexible and adaptive structure with a clear set of stages and milestones that we can measure as we move from emerging-level through practitioner-level and into expert-level UDL adoption (see Novak and Rodriguez 2018).

UDL Champions: The University of Nebraska–Lincoln

Julia Remsik Larsen, Grace Troupe, and Ash Mitchell are instructional designers in the College of Education and Human Sciences at the University of Nebraska–Lincoln. I spoke with them about how they have adopted UDL across all undergraduate programs. Julia shared how it all started:

> I had a department chair come to me with a request to start looking at accessibility in the courses in his department. It was supposed to be just a little pilot: just looking at a couple of courses and doing an accessibility audit. That was in fall of 2019. In spring of 2020, the pandemic hit, so this project got put on the back burner—which ended up being a helpful thing in terms of being able to promote the ideas of accessibility and UDL to the larger campus audience. . . .
>
> In January of 2021, we got a request from an instructor who was really frustrated because they had received a [disability] accommodation letter, but it didn't say how to do any of the things for the student. We restarted this idea of the audits, but instead of doing accessibility audits in classrooms, we turned it into a resource where we could direct instructors: Here are the basics you need to know; here is how to apply the UDL principles. This was really successful. It ended up being a multi-unit collaboration across the university, with our Services for Students with Disabilities (SSD) office, our Institutional Equity and Compliance office, Information Technology Services, the libraries, and the Diversity and Inclusion office.

> At first, this project was led by our unit's instructional designers. Our director and associate director were both incredibly supportive. They lent their titles to the cause: When we would reach out to new units to bring them on board, we could say "our director has asked us to do these things."

Grace then explained how this campus-wide effort grew from a passion project for one campus leader to now being a required element in the curriculum across eight schools at the university.

> After we created the Canvas course [learning management system] resource on accommodations and UDL, a colleague in IT who had created a ten-minute "A Little Bit about Accessibility" resource approached us and asked us to make a more robust training using our institution's training software, called Bridge. Accessibility has always been the door that we open wider to bring in UDL; once we finished designing a one-hour training, we wanted to find units to pilot it. Our director asked us to present at our Academic Solutions Council (all of the assistant deans of Teaching and Learning).
>
> We painted the picture of how many students use the accommodations process; while only 5 percent of students are registered with our SSD office, we also know that two-thirds of students with disabilities are not receiving formal accommodations. So, closer to 20 percent of our students actually need support. Not only that, but following the pandemic, one out of ten people who got COVID have cognitive dysfunctions associated with long COVID. The numbers keep getting bigger and bigger, but our staff and budget remain the same.

> We hear sometimes "I don't have any students with disabilities" from instructors, when we know that they are definitely there. We made the case for who needs support, who else benefits (nearly all of our learners), and how the challenge is largely invisible. Instead of just a few pilots, all of the deans said yes.

The experience of the instructional design team at the University of Nebraska–Lincoln highlights patterns that many of us in higher education are noting today. There has been a groundswell of interest among individual instructors to help lower barriers and make our learning interactions more equitable. We're also seeing some of our existing support systems for learners—units like our disability-support, mental-health, library, and academic-counseling services—stretching to try to serve more and more people despite static funding and staffing levels.

That's Not All, Folks

Ash Mitchell at the University of Nebraska–Lincoln sums up this part of our book well. She talks about how, even though her university now has required training in UDL methods across all undergraduate programs, her team collectively feels that they are only in the middle of the UDL adoption process.

> There still needs to be more for us. It's very much a journey. Bringing all of those campus groups together helped us better understand what was possible. Everyone was doing their own pieces, but there wasn't great communication across all of the units that were affected by the proposed changes. There wasn't a clear picture of

> the landscape, so this collaboration allowed us to develop materials and processes to have in place before we said to instructors, "we know you are stressed and have no time; this is where we'd like you to prioritize your efforts." If we spend one hour training everyone in how to make content and interactions more open and accessible in the first place, this is a low time cost that has a huge savings over time in terms of remediation and re-work.

The adoption of UDL principles does not require everyone on campus to become UDL experts or to invest significant time and resources into completely shifting or changing our collective practices. Rather, campus leaders should aim to support everyone in the entire organization to take one or two concrete steps to lower barriers, increase access, and empower learners to act on their own behalf within our various systems. In chapter 2, you will learn (a) how we can reframe UDL for higher-education audiences and needs, (b) what kinds of groundwork make a campus-wide UDL implementation even possible, and (c) a five-part set of shifts that we can enact in order to set achievable and clear expectations for our UDL adoption efforts.

2

FRAME UDL FOR HIGHER EDUCATION

Now that you have some background about the how universal design for learning (UDL) came to higher education, it's time to begin framing your conversations with colleagues who will become part of your scale-up efforts. In chapter 2, we'll talk about why UDL is a mission-focused approach to the design of learning interactions across campus, address some hidden (and often incorrect) assumptions about UDL, craft a narrative for adopting UDL in higher education, and establish five shifts in our collective actions that support three strategic pillars that are themselves aligned to our mission, vision, and shared values.

The biggest question this book seeks to answer is "why should we adopt UDL at our institution?" There are a number of possible answers, all of which are compelling. UDL supports our commitments to social justice in the design of our curricula and services. UDL helps us to be proactive in including and supporting learners and employees from diverse life circumstances. UDL is an evidence-based approach to the entire design, teaching, and assessment cycle that allows us to meet the criteria to which our accrediting bodies hold us accountable. None of these arguments, however, tends to sway our boards of trustees, presidents, and other campus leaders. Rather, the frame within which I want to explore UDL with you is simpler: UDL helps our bottom line.

UDL Is Good Business

If for no other reason, we should be adopting UDL across our entire institutions—from the classroom to the support staff to the leadership teams—because designing learning interactions with multiple ways to engage, get information, and take action is a fiscally sound approach to being wise stewards of our resources. Let's unpack this approach, do a little myth-busting and reframing, and then talk about five ways to build a campus-wide UDL program on the solid foundations of our existing policies and practices.

In the nearly three decades since UDL became widespread, first among our K–12 colleagues and more recently in higher education, we've seen adoption of UDL practices hover around 10 percent of most populations of instructors, staff members, and campus leaders. Why hasn't UDL grown to scale yet? Examining this question will help you to frame UDL and respond to questions and concerns from your colleagues as you begin your UDL-at-scale journey.

Unpacking Some Hidden Assumptions

First, there are some unexamined K–12-environment-specific assumptions that are baked into the three principles, nine guidelines, and thirty-six considerations of UDL. Using recent evidence and research from higher-education practitioners and theorists, we can simplify and "translate" the UDL guidelines and considerations to broaden their applicability for higher-education systemic uses. As they are structured now, UDL's thirty-six considerations assume a few things that are common in K–12 learning environments. Some of these features carry over nearly unchanged when we situate UDL in higher education, but a few of them need to be reexamined or reframed for a higher-education implementation.

UDL currently assumes that primary learning interactions occur in a physical classroom space. While there have been several studies about UDL in online teaching and learning, the language in the UDL considerations themselves privilege real-time, colocated instruction and learning. You'll find references to "the classroom," the process of "schooling," and even a few sample techniques specific to an in-classroom K–12 experience, such as the advice to "provide sentence starters or sentence strips" (short pieces of paper with sample sentence elements on them, with a blank space for students to complete the sentences) as a way to implement UDL Consideration 5.2, "Use multiple tools for construction and composition" (CAST 2024b).

For higher-education UDL practitioners, we need to do some translating for our circumstances, where we expect learners will spend roughly equal amounts of effort on their own in preparation and practice as they do when they are with us in our classrooms and lab environments. We also need to do some translating when we think about hybrid, synchronous remote, and online asynchronous teaching and learning, where we ask learners to exercise a significant amount of executive function and self-direction.

The UDL guidelines also silently assume a power imbalance between instructors and learners. In K–12 environments, teachers work with learners who are still in the early stages of developing their social, emotional, and intellectual capacities, so the exercise of power and control in the classroom is a necessary part of maintaining order and focus. In higher education, we cannot assume instructors will exercise control and power, nor can we be certain that respect for instructors is automatically given by learners.

There is already a mountain of evidence that college students vary in their response to instructors based on the instructors' gender, ethnicity, affect, and a host of other personal attributes (see Pittman and Tobin 2022). Fortunately, higher-education institutions can build on existing instructor-support systems to recognize instructor variability as well as learner variability (we'll pick up this idea again in the next chapter).

A third assumption in the UDL guidelines is the conflation of the roles of designers and instructors. In K–12 spaces, the majority of teachers are responsible for designing their own lessons, using state and national standards and outcomes as frames within which they can exercise considerable academic freedom in designing and teaching. For example, even in statewide K–12 UDL efforts such as the New Hampshire UDL Innovation Network (New Hampshire Department of Education 2019), while entire schools get trained on UDL principles and techniques, the assumption is individual teachers will work on "their" UDL implementations, sharing good ideas with their peers, but ultimately responsible for only their own classrooms.

Conversely, in higher education, while the "you made it, you teach it" model remains common, we can no longer assume the people or teams who designed given learning experiences—from class activities through course designs all the way to program development—will be the same people who will teach using those materials and designs. Codesigned and "master shell" course designs are common enough to break the assumption of a single person designing and teaching from given materials. This situation makes a strong argument for the adoption of UDL principles and strategies in higher education. Designing the materials and plans for interaction in an inclusive way helps to lower barriers more systematically for large groups of learners—and for their instructors, too.

Framing UDL for At-Scale Adoption in Higher Education

Each of the nine guidelines and thirty-six considerations in the UDL framework is underpinned by evidence-based research, and we have now reached a critical point where studies in higher education are starting to support and interrogate the efficacy of all thirty-six considerations for higher-education audiences and contexts. By keeping the three primary principles of UDL intact (multiple means of engagement, representation, and action/expression), we can update and remix the guidelines and considerations of the UDL framework to encompass new research results, address assumptions, and apply to a broader range of higher- education learning and design experiences.

As seen in table 2.1, the current grid of the UDL framework crosses the three principles of engagement, representation, and action/expression against broad stages in the learning process (access, support, and executive function) in order to create nine UDL guidelines, in which we and our learners design options for "recruiting interest, sustaining effort & persistence, self-regulation, perception, language & symbols, comprehension, physical action,

TABLE 2.1 The Nine Universal Design for Learning Guidelines. Adapted from https://udlguidelines.cast.org/

	Design multiple means of engagement	*Design multiple means of representation*	*Design multiple means of action & expression*
Access	G7: Welcoming interest & identities	G1: Perception	G4: Interaction
Support	G8: Sustaining effort & persistence	G2: Language & symbols	G5: Expression & communication
Executive Function	G9: Emotional Capacity	G3: Building knowledge	G6: Strategy Development

expression & communication, and executive functions" (CAST 2024a).

A good example of a remixed set of UDL considerations for at-scale higher-education application is shown in table 2.2, created by Sonya Woods at Penn State University (personal communication 2022). The three core principles of UDL remain at the top of the grid: design multiple means of engagement, representation, and action & expression.

In the remix for instructional designers, the "access, support, and executive function" processes morph into "orient/onboard, personalize, and reflect" to recognize that college and university learners are better able to support their own learning and engage in self-directed learning activities once they understand the scope and structure of the learning environment (although even as adults, we're not yet 100% good at it—think of the last time you asked for more time on a research article or collaborative project with coworkers). Each of these new row labels intersects more closely with established workflows and effective practices among our instructional-design colleagues. CAST's original approach assumes that classroom instructors will design their own learning interactions. Woods's revisions shift the focus from individual

TABLE 2.2 A Modified Set of Universal Design for Learning Guidelines for Instructional Designers (Woods, 2022).

	Design multiple means of engagement	*Design multiple means of representation*	*Design multiple means of action & expression*
Orient/ Onboard	G7: Recruit interest	G1: Perception	G4: Physical action
Personalize	G8: Sustain effort & persistence	G2: Language & symbols	G5: Expression & communication
Reflect	G9: Self-regulation	G3: Comprehension	G6: Executive functions

instructors working solo to the work that institutions do collaboratively to support learner agency—the work that we do at scale.

The shift from "access" on the part of the learner to "orient/onboard" actions on the part of instructional designers in Woods's model reframes the focus to helping learners to find available support tools and people, learn about the culture of the organization, and understand the affordances of the learning environment. We also shift from how learners "build" their own understanding of learning experiences to how designers "personalize" learning environments—offering multipath choices, contextual cues and hints, and purposeful opportunities for collaboration, reflection, and learner-generated content. The bottom row changes from how learners internalize strategies to how designers create intentional spaces for learners to reflect on their experiences. We design experiences that guide learners to engage in metacognition in order to manage risk, make the structures for support more explicit, and actively design spaces and activities that call learners in as part of the community of the class, course, department, institution, and field of study. Notice how the nine guidelines themselves retain their labels, but in our at-scale model, we broaden the agency to include learners, designers, instructors, and institutions. What does this shift allow us to do at scale that we might not be able to do at an individual level?

UDL at the Micro, Meso, and Macro Scales

Because the focus of UDL is learning—how individuals engage with, take in, and practice with ideas—until now, we've designed from the individual learner outward, using patterns within the variable ways that people learn to create small group-level structures that support learning. This is the highest level "design multiple means" understanding of UDL. As I've argued above, the practiced focus of higher education is, perhaps surprisingly, not learning but *instruction.* John Tagg persuasively argues in *The Instruction Myth* (2019) that our schools, colleges, and universities are set up to track and measure how much instruction has taken place: We measure credit hours, seat time, and progress through curricula as denoted by grades. Few of these measures tell us where learners started in their understanding and how far they have come in their learning. Rather, we're best at saying which students are good at navigating the processes of our institutions.

In order for UDL to offer us value, we should be able to point to how its adoption across our varied and often decentralized systems of support, instruction, and assessment helps our learners to stick with us more effectively. Indeed, over the past few years, we have seen many new large-scale studies that show how inclusive design, writ large, creates cultural and structural cues that silently nudge instructors, support staff members, and administrators toward acting in more inclusive ways by default. This is something of a "Trojan horse" argument. By designing systems and processes using the UDL principles, guidelines, and considerations, we bring learners closer to our stated goals of increased student persistence, retention, and satisfaction.

We have been collectively moving in this direction for a while, creating structures that suggest ways to specify and measure a framework that is predicated on flexibility and variability. Katie Novak and Kristan Rodriguez created the *UDL Progression Rubric* (2018) to show how individual instructor-designers could implement the nine UDL guidelines and (at the time) thirty-one UDL checkpoints in instructor-led ("emerging"), structured but learner-agentic ("proficient"), and multipath ("progressing toward expert practice") ways. This creates measurable levels for UDL implementation by individual learning designers. When we think about UDL at scale, we want similarly to expand the design in our entire systems beyond the plus-one, "here are some choices, so choose one," starting points where so many of our colleges and universities are now.

In essence, the at-scale frame of UDL looks a lot like the individual learner-access practices with which UDL began many decades ago, now applied in their broadest possible methods. The goal of UDL at scale is to get beyond what we might call "mere access" by designing entire systems and ways of operating that presuppose agency, voice, choice, safety, and belonging for everyone involved in our institutions—learners, instructors, support staff, and administrators.

Setting the Stage for Success: Five Shifts

Now that we have framed UDL at scale in terms of designing systems, processes, policies, and practices to be more flexible and inclusive, let's start thinking about what UDL at scale might actually look like in your institution. I propose five shifts in how we think about UDL when we apply it to our entire institutions.

1. **We adopt fewer, broader, more strategic goals**, and we measure them in terms of overall learner persistence, retention, and satisfaction.
2. **Individual applications give way to systemic practices.** Instead of making changes one at a time and repeating them person to person, course to course, or service to service, we change the structures themselves, so that everyone adheres to simpler but broader inclusive techniques.
3. **We harness the power of defaults.** It's amazing how few colleagues raise a fist and cry "you can't make me do that; I have academic freedom" when everyone follows inclusive practices because of the ways systems and services are designed.

4. **Our efforts move beyond the classroom** and formal teaching-and-learning interactions. We start to think of the entire ecosystem of the institution and identify where learning is happening during learners' time away from our formal learning spaces and when they are working alongside support staffers like librarians, tutors, counselors, and so on.
5. **We weigh academic freedom against access & predictability.** Part of lowering barriers for learners is not making them learn new patterns, systems, and ways of being when they move from one part of our environment to another.

Let's examine each of these five scaling-up ideas in turn and talk about what UDL looks like through these lenses.

Shift 1: We adopt fewer, broader, more strategic goals. Imagine a stadium filled with proud families at a graduation ceremony. College graduates in their caps and gowns wave to their loved ones. One graduate holds his diploma cover aloft. This is the image we love to share as campus leaders: successful graduates. When we talk with our campus audiences about the impact of adopting UDL and other inclusive-design approaches, we should definitely *not* start with the thirty-six UDL considerations. Rather, our conversation focuses on fewer, broader, more strategic goals. Starting with the detail-level information about UDL subtly encourages colleagues to focus on the individual tasks that they can perform, rather than on the general outcomes to which everyone in your organization should contribute. Keep the focus on what can be done collectively and consistently. For example, talk about UDL in terms of learner persistence, retention, and satisfaction.

- **UDL increases learner persistence.** More students who are there on day one are still there to complete the final examination or turn in their course project. We know that UDL has a positive effect on persistence because of large-scale research at individual schools (e.g., Davies, Schelly and Spooner 2013), as well as meta-analyses of the literature across smaller-scale studies (Capp 2017).
- **UDL increases learner retention.** More learners take a course with me and then return next term to continue their educations with you. We know that UDL increases student retention (see Tobin 2014)—the holy grail of every provost and registrar—because of its positive effect on what's often called the "freshman cliff," where students enter their studies but then drop out for various reasons. By lowering barriers and normalizing help-seeking behaviors, UDL at scale affects student retention numbers.
- **UDL increases learner satisfaction.** Study after study shows that learners who feel strong senses of belonging, choice, control, safety, and agency are more than five times as likely to be satisfied with their experiences in colleges and universities (Al-Azawei, Parslow and Lundqvist 2017). Not only do satisfied students stick with us in greater numbers, but they are also more likely to advocate that others study with us. This impact of UDL, especially when it is adopted as part of a larger push for equitable and inclusive education, is the most easily measured at scale with student-rating and exit-interview instruments.

Shift 2: Individual applications give way to systemic practices. Imagine that there are twenty steps to perfecting UDL (there aren't, but think along with me for a moment). Most of our efforts to date have been to train a small, willing group of colleagues to reach step twenty, while the majority of our instructors, staff members, and administrators remain at step one. When we think about UDL at scale, we design our systems and aim our advocacy efforts toward getting everyone in the institution to step two. We allocate money, time, talent, and political capital toward these efforts at the level of the entire organization, with the push for change coming from the top down, rather than solely as grassroots efforts.

Shift 3: We harness the power of defaults. It's not effective when one department or office does the work of lowering access barriers for learners, and then the learners encounter another department or office where barriers still exist. Learners can get even more frustrated with inconsistent experiences than if barriers were consistently in place. It's dispiriting to have a brief experience of easier and smoother going, and then to drop right back into more challenging environments and structures. UDL requires near-perfect adoption if it is to be most effective.

Reminding people, training people, pleading with them to remember to practice inclusive techniques consistently is doomed to be ever only a partial solution to a challenge like that. There are already whole shelves worth of legal requirements related to making materials accessible, and yet colleges and universities continue to be sued for our inaccessible materials—because the work happens unevenly across our institutions. Oh, everyone agrees that taking the time to make things accessible is the right thing to do. Many people look at the sheer enormity of retrofitting all our existing inaccessible content and suffer from "analysis paralysis," and don't even start.

Rather than trusting everyone to do the right thing, assign resources to create systems that just require good practices. For example, require descriptive alt text for images uploaded into your learning management system (LMS), or create a workflow in your media-services area requiring staff to create captions for all video content produced through that office. This part of UDL at scale helps to normalize the work of making engagement, representation, and action choices. It moves accessibility and inclusion from "extra effort" to "everyday tasks." For example, in 2023 Marc Thompson and his team in the Center for Innovation in Teaching & Learning (CITL) at the University of Illinois Urbana–Champaign created a UDL team tasked with making "inclusivity and accessibility more integral to the course design and delivery process, and thereby, improve student-learning outcomes and quality of instruction" (Adams 2023). Rather than trust that everyone on campus will follow the guidance of the CITL staff, the UDL team created default conditions that everyone follows automatically by updating their course-development quality indicators: "CITL course quality criteria like the Core Elements of Online Course Quality incorporate UDL principles and aim to engage all students in their respective optimal learning experiences" (Yan 2023).

In the next chapter, we will return to the idea of crafting defaults as a UDL practice. While most of the approaches and strategies in this book can be mixed, rearranged, and modified, the experiences of dozens of schools, colleges, and universities suggests there is one best way to design default conditions: start with the general-education offerings. Your general-education or core curriculum is the collection of offerings that all learners must experience; the gen-eds are the foundations on which all your credentials are built. As such, gen-ed courses are more likely to be collaboratively designed, and they have the largest reach and impact on learners across your institution. Because the gen-eds are nearly always designed "by committee," the content, structure, and progression of these courses are typically heavily supplemented with instructor-guide or teaching-notes content. It is these guides for instructors that create the default conditions for teaching and facilitating the learner interactions in the gen-ed courses.

Shift 4: Our efforts move beyond the classroom. While UDL had its beginnings in the classroom, it is a framework for lowering barriers across various learning interactions in which our campuses engage. And there are a lot of learning interactions happening in spaces far beyond the classroom, lab, and lecture hall. Advisors are teaching students how to navigate the systems of our colleges and universities. Tutoring staff members are teaching study skills. Mental health counselors are teaching coping strategies. Librarians are teaching how to assess and work with information.

Wherever students interact with support services, think of how these engagements are teaching and learning interactions. If students are learning something—even if it's not part of the academic curriculum—we can apply the principles of UDL to lower barriers, increase engagement, and support learner voice, choice, and agency. A good example of this shift in action is the strategic priority expressed by the yearly EDUCAUSE "Top Ten" list of priorities for campus information technology (IT) teams, one of which was recently "meet students where they are: provide universal access to institutional services" (Bedi, et al. 2024). Institutions collectively want

> to shape a more expansive approach toward institutional services and a greater commitment to help students overcome their individual barriers to academic success. Leaders are introducing or expanding services to address food and housing insecurity, childcare, transportation, mental health, career counseling, and basic technology needs. Many instructors and instructional technologists see this time as

> an opportunity to invest in universal design for learning, or UDL. Ultimately, universal access entails providing multi-modal channels to accessing individualized services. (Bedi, et al. 2024)

Shift 5: We weigh academic freedom against access and predictability. Finally, at scale, we have to balance the competing interests of academic freedom against access and predictability for learners. Our instructors have the right to teach their fields in the manner they deem best: that's the essence of academic freedom. As we think about UDL at scale, we should be especially wary of framing UDL as a set of prescriptive actions that forces instructors all to do exactly the same thing. Yes, UDL is all about optimizing choices, so it's doubly ironic to say "you must" when we're talking about the content, knowledge, and skills in the fields we teach and the services we provide.

At the same time, we absolutely should say "you must" when it comes to making our various systems predictable, such as using the same color schemes, general layouts, button styles, and text names for common controls across our websites, LMS, and other touchpoints. This goes beyond the identity manual and glossary that your marketing team has created, and speaks to having federated style, vocabulary, and operational parameters for all the base systems on which people build.

Your information technology, or IT, colleagues are your allies in this conversation. By the way, we already have predictable systems for our physical environments. They're called classrooms, and they all look and operate roughly the same, except for labs and other special-needs situations. A splendid example is the work that the University of Cincinnati has done to customize all its student-facing tools to have the same look and feel. They started with an electronic accessibility policy (2020) and worked outward from those guiding principles. Along the way, they discovered that UDL was a framework that fit all the needs that their policy expressed. Especially because some colleagues can mistake consistent and predictable access to systems and tools for an encroachment on academic freedom (it's not), it's important for UDL at scale that we get support for those requirements from the administration, faculty senate, academic-staff governance, and any other campus oversight bodies.

Three Strategic Pillars

Once we understand the five conceptual shifts outlined above, we can create a top-level frame for our UDL-at-scale efforts, resting our arguments on three strategic pillars: access, inclusion, and predictability. Let's examine why these are the right ways to lead a UDL approach at scale, using my own university's vision statement and its expression in our strategic framework documents (UW–Madison 2019).

Strategic Pillar 1: Access. The first strategic priority that UDL at scale addresses is access. Imagine a graduate student in the library stacks, using his wheelchair to get around. Think of students commuting to campus who have work and caregiving responsibilities in addition to their studies. Think of remote learners, of students with military commitments—there are a lot of reasons why access is a concept that guides our entire institutions. In the University of Wisconsin–Madison's strategic plan, we find the following ideas:

Excellence in Teaching & Educational Achievement

- Provide access to a world-class, affordable educational experience.
- Expand access to a UW-Madison education, leveraging new modes of delivery to engage with students throughout their lives.

Excellence in Research & Scholarship

- Provide a modern research support structure that fosters innovation, promotes interdisciplinary collaboration, and drives discovery on future research challenges. (UW–Madison 2019)

This is the sort of whole-institution language that you can find, quote, and align with your UDL message. For instance, at UW–Madison, they're all about providing and expanding "access to a world-class, affordable educational experience"—it's right there in their vision statement.

Strategic Pillar 2: Inclusion. UDL also aligns with the inclusion priorities of our institutions. Even in places where terms like "diversity" and "inclusion" are frowned upon, nearly all of our colleges and universities talk about making the institution reflect the community around it in terms of its composition, aims, culture, and goals. A good example of this more neutral stance is the "Wisconsin Idea" that goes back to the founding of the University of Wisconsin: the university should be serving the entire state with its offerings.

Living the Wisconsin Idea

- Share the benefits of a world-class teaching and research university throughout Wisconsin and beyond our borders.

A Vibrant Campus Community

- Enhance the holistic development of students by combining learning in and out of the classroom that is steeped in the values of the university.

- Enhance diversity among our students, faculty, and staff.
- Build upon our strong commitment to diversity to create a welcoming, empowered, and inclusive community. (UW–Madison 2019)

Inclusion has been part of our university's goals right from the start, so inclusion is a natural argument for adopting UDL ideas at scale. Here again, the language that we use to describe UDL's goals mirrors those already adopted by the institution and helps us to show alignment to the institution's priorities, like attracting a culturally diverse student body.

Strategic Pillar 3: Predictability. Predictability can take many forms in our campus mission and vision. Our learners—and our employees—benefit from having "learn them once" systems in place for study and for professional learning. All of us can then devote more energy to the challenges of the subjects we're studying or supporting rather than to learning new systems and tools at every step.

Excellence in Teaching & Educational Achievement

- Strengthen educational outcomes, career development, and the college experience for all students.

A High-Performing Organization

- Strengthen our financial performance, growing revenues, controlling costs, and delivering new and innovative ways to invest in our strategic priorities, while maintaining a commitment to the highest ethical standards. (UW–Madison 2019)

Predictability can be a tricky part of large-scale UDL to tie in to existing organizational vision and strategy, so look for the language about strengthening financial performance and educational outcomes. That's code for "be more efficient," which means having standardized structures, tools, and practices rather than each silo on campus doing its own thing.

If your campus is mostly silo and hardly any "all together," this makes the argument for UDL predictability especially enticing to leadership—and especially fretful for the folks in the departments and units. By focusing our arguments on outcomes for learners, we are better positioned to get buy-in from all the stakeholders in the conversation: instructors, staff members, and leadership.

Simple Versus Complex

So far in this book, I've been arguing about how UDL's three principles and nine guidelines can help us to increase learners' access and to support learner variability. Because scaling up requires us to focus on only a few key ideas and practices, you might read this entire book and think "ah, UDL is easier than I thought. We can make a checklist of UDL actions and have everybody do them across all of our units and departments."

And you could easily stop there. I'll encourage you, though, as you read further, to create intentional space in your scaling-up program for supporting at least a few folks in your college or university—perhaps your UDL champions, as we'll discuss in later chapters—to dive more deeply into the nuances and complexities of UDL as a design framework that can be applied in myriad ways to reduce barriers and support students proactively, while also allowing us to enact asset-based pedagogies.

Especially at the level of the thirty-six UDL considerations, the UDL framework can leverage students' assets, acknowledge their backgrounds and experiences, align to their strengths and abilities, and address their preferences and interests. For instance, in designing online and technology-mediated learning activities, more advanced UDL ideas can help us with the chunking of content and interactions, selection of synchronous and asynchronous alternatives for information and communication, provision of mastery-oriented feedback, and teaching learners how to use features of digital tools (see Rao 2021). None of these are skills that should be included in scaled-up UDL-adoption projects. They are simultaneously necessary for some of the design and teaching resources at your institution.

As you read the rest of the book, know that while we will be exploring how to simplify the actions everyone in your organization should take together, you should not forget to make a place for more detailed study and application, as well. UDL is not a laundry list of practices to apply piecemeal. Rather, it is a comprehensive framework for designing learning engagements that support a wide variety of learners.

A Call to Action

As campus leaders, we hear arguments in favor of many different courses of action, and it falls to us to decide which ideas have merit, and then to prioritize those that most benefit our institutions, communities, employees, and students. UDL has historically been a difficult "sell" in higher education because its very flexibility is difficult to repeat, compare, and measure in the ways we're used to doing in major projects at our colleges and universities.

As you've seen in this chapter, UDL helps us with bottom-line budget-and-enrollment concerns. We can reframe the UDL that many of us know from the work of our colleagues in the K–12 educational world so that it fits better into the less regimented and more atomized work environment of higher-education institutions. By shifting to an "onboard/orient, personalize, reflect" way of describing the UDL guidelines, we set up five shifts in how we frame our use of UDL principles.

1. We adopt fewer, broader, more strategic goals.
2. Individual applications give way to systemic practices.
3. We harness the power of defaults.
4. Our efforts move beyond the classroom.
5. We weigh academic freedom against access & predictability.

These shifts allow us then to zoom all the way out and build our UDL efforts on three strategic pillars that align with our existing institutional mission, vision, values, and goals—access, inclusion, and predictability.

As you think about the conceptual framing in this chapter, what actions will you take to help start, evolve, or spread the conversation at your institution to create systems, practices, and policies that provide flexibility and lower barriers for your learners, instructors, staff, administrators, and community? Once you have that list, continue to the next chapter, where we'll detail the components of a successful UDL-at-scale adoption and examine some common pitfalls to watch out for along the way.

3

CREATE CONDITIONS THAT MAKE UDL POSSIBLE

Whether your institution has a long history of universal design for learning (UDL) implementations—by individuals or groups of instructors—or you're just starting with the UDL framework in order to lower access barriers across your organization, UDL at scale is made much more challenging, if not impossible, if the conditions that support inclusive-design work aren't present. In this chapter, you'll find practical ways to create space, time, and incentives for your entire organization to become a UDL campus.

The Return on Our UDL Investment

I've worked with many colleges and universities who want to lower access barriers for their learners, and by far the most common question I hear has to do with the return on their investment of time: learning about the UDL framework, examining their current learning designs, and applying UDL principles where they find the most persistent barriers and gaps for learners. "That sounds like an awful lot of work. What will we get out of all this effort?" My response can sound paradoxical: yes, UDL is indeed a lot of work, if you're doing it alone, late, or at a surface level.

As campus leaders, we can unthinkingly add to the workload of our instructors with new policies and requirements, even well-intentioned ones. When we put the onus for making learning experiences more engaging, accessible, and responsive solely on the shoulders of instructors and we do not at the same time remove other responsibilities from their workloads, we create conditions under which only those with motivation, privilege, open time, and/or individual incentive will be able to take part in the effort. This is, unfortunately, the most common scenario under which our colleges and universities expect to see change happen around access barriers. We train our instructors in a design framework like UDL with a one-hour workshop, and then we ask them all to apply it (see King-Sears, et al. 2023).

What we get in such situations mirrors the unspoken assumption in the "that's a lot of work" statement that I hear so often. Too few people seem interested, and those who do take action are often applying the principles of UDL in limited ways where they perceive the biggest "pinch points" in their learners' experiences of the work in question. Starting with the pinch points is a strategy I advise often, but it is meant to be a starting point for individual action, not the entirety of the action itself.

In this chapter, we'll unpack three key "step zero" elements that need to be in place, or at least robustly developing, for UDL to take root across your entire campus: accessible tools and materials, available instructional support resources, and time for everyone involved to focus on UDL.

Step 0.1: Accessible Materials

Accessibility is a foundation on which to build access. Let's unpack that sentence. If our materials and tools do not provide accessible options, it is difficult to take actions to lower access barriers, which is the goal of UDL. The first and most fundamental condition for implementing UDL at scale is ensuring that your entire organization is using and creating accessible content and materials. We can avoid the "analysis paralysis" that can set in when we look at the sheer enormity of retrofitting all our existing websites, course materials, and so on. Rather than try to redo decades of work, work with your shared-governance campus partners to set a date on the calendar after which all campus units who create content and materials will adopt a minimum set of accessibility parameters.

For web-based content, this often takes the form of the Web Content Accessibility Guidelines (WCAG) international standard (World Wide Web Consortium 2022). For materials created or selected by your campus, the National Center on Accessible Educational Materials (NCAEM) has created a set of quality indicators for providing accessible materials (NCAEM 2020) across an entire campus. The idea behind starting with "mere accessibility" is to create a workflow that moves the training and practice of making accessible content away from "extra" work into the mindset of doing necessary work that until now we had been broadly missing, with the eventual end state of accessible content creation becoming part of the everyday work in which all of our units engage.

A good example of a scaled-up accessible materials program is the California State University system's Accessible Technology Initiative, or ATI (California State University 2024). Carl Schottmiller in the Center for Effective Teaching and Learning at the California State University, Los Angeles describes the history and process of growing the ATI program to maturity:

> The California State University system has an Accessible Technology Initiative. This initiative's mission is to make information technology resources and services accessible to all. Each campus has their own localized ATI working

> group. In 2023, the California State University Chancellor's Office audited Cal State LA for campus accessibility compliance. The audit sought to ascertain the effectiveness of operational and administrative controls, and ensure compliance with relevant regulations. Cal State LA needs a campus procedure to ensure compliance. Our goal was to establish the procedure by June 30, 2024. We needed collaboration across divisions to create a campus-wide procedure. Our Accessible Instructional Materials (AIM) process is an Academic Affairs initiative to make digital instructional materials, starting in Fall 2024 courses, 100% accessible. (Schottmiller 2024)

The AIM process at Cal State LA began by assigning design, accessibility, and media resources to those courses in which students had requested disability accommodations. Once that became part of the established workflow on campus, these people applied their experience to create a standard process for making materials accessible in all courses offered by the university. This creates a solid foundation on which to expand into UDL.

Similarly, Anna Greene, Carrie Hansel, Michael Mace, and their colleagues at Indiana University (IU) recently led a university-wide effort to adopt digital accessibility techniques to make materials available across the various service areas of the institution. I enjoyed talking with these three campus leaders about their efforts to make materials more accessible, and their approach initially surprised me: they didn't start with the materials at all. Relying on James Clear's advice in *Atomic Habits* that "you do not rise to the level of your goals; you fall to the level of your systems" (Clear 2018, 27), Mike Mace talked about the IU team beginning by "putting in systems that promote accessibility and provide tools, talent, and training for accessibility at the point of need—versus, you know, reactive [responses]. So, what we're really trying to do is move from a reactive point of accommodation to a proactive point of accessibility" (personal communication 15 Nov. 2023). The argument for putting resources in place to create "born-accessible" materials as a matter of systemic or everyday effort came during the COVID-19 pandemic in 2020 and 2021, when, as Carrie Hansel told me,

> The biggest thing was the realization that the accommodation process is broken. A lot of our faculty [members] who had never touched the learning management system (especially in our main campus), were forced into delivering e-learning and never had done it before. They were immediately thrust into the digital realm, which just showed how a lot of that digital realm is broken: our publisher tools, learning technology, and knowledge of accessibility aren't where we need to be.
>
> We were doing a lot of work one time, for one student, and that would just get thrown out the window. Even in one class, you would have, statistically, four, five, ten (depending on how big the course is) additional students who would have a print or learning impairment that lost any kind of benefit from the work that we were doing for that one student, one time.
>
> Our big question became how can we make it so we're fixing these in place, and then is it reusable for all students? We wanted to avoid reinventing the wheel, and that was what drove our shift to ePub as our primary document format. We no longer offer a menu of options: Our students are going to see ePub when they are with the university. We're trying to use as much of the assistive technology that's built into the systems that they use already. (personal communication 15 Nov. 2023)

As the team at Indiana University discovered, discerning broad patterns in the demand for accessible materials can help your campus to identify ways to provide access alternatives for content from the start. Once these patterns and needs are identified, it's time to engage in the next part of creating the conditions for making UDL possible: staffing and support.

Step 0.2: Instructional Support Resources

Ideally, our campus budgets shift and evolve in response to immediate needs (maintaining our physical buildings, for example), planned goals (growing to support a large incoming class of students), and emerging trends (shifting resources to support more technology-mediated learning spaces). In practice, and despite all our talk of "constant evolution" and "innovation culture," what we spend our money on changes remarkably little from year to year. If you have access to your college or university's annual report (or, even better, the actual budget documents), compare the share of funds spent each year on employee salaries/benefits, physical infrastructure, academic support, student support, technology, and research/public service. These are, in descending order, the largest—and most stable—categories of expenditures among colleges and universities year over year (National Center for Educational Statistics 2023).

As campus leaders, we can identify gaps and opportunities without being able to direct significant resources to address them. Hence our deferred-maintenance plans about the leaking rec-center roof, the disturbing but economical pattern of replacing tenure-line full-time faculty members with contingent and adjunct instructors, and not replacing budget lines when staff members retire or projects are completed. In our current general climate of "do more with less," how—and why—should we prioritize our scarce resources to accessibility efforts?

In the most common accessibility-across-campus scenario today, a campus unit, usually the teaching and learning center or the disability-support team, sponsors a series of workshops or talks that are open to all instructors about how to "do accessibility." Attendees learn the reasons behind making things accessible from the start, and are also trained in basic accessibility methods, such as using the semantic heading structure in word-processed and web-based materials. These efforts largely fail to achieve the breadth of practice for which they are designed, for three important reasons.

One, they are seldom required of everyone on campus, so only those with existing interest in—or privilege and time to study—accessible methods usually attend. Adjunct instructors and support staffers rarely have the luxury of coming to these programs. Two, efforts to train individual employees are a mismatch for the goal: we will never be able to "individual effort" our way past system-level concerns. And three, pitching accessibility as the responsibility of instructors alone creates another unfunded mandate that adds to the workload of a population in our campus communities that is already feeling overloaded.

Adequate staffing levels for information technology (IT), media, design, and teaching-and-learning support areas make good business sense. When interested instructors come to the media-services team and request, say, help in creating flipped classroom designs, if our media staffers are trained in accessible methods and have accessibility as part of their everyday workflows, their response is "sure, we'll send a camera team to your classroom—and we'll help you break up the video into four-minute segments and help with the captions, too. That's just what we do here."

Because our budgets seldom provide large pots of unassigned funds that we might use to staff up support areas to handle the core work of accessibility, we can use other levers to establish practice patterns that lead to cultural change and then budgetary change. In other words, we move away from seeing accessible practices as add-ons to the work of our instructors toward a view of accessibility as a core element of our everyday operations across all the service areas of our campuses. Two examples can serve to highlight how this sort of shift can happen at your institution.

One of the largest expenses that supports instruction on our campuses is the learning management system (LMS) and the related constellations of technology and media tools that are supported by our IT teams. Many colleges and universities worldwide decide which tools and systems they will purchase and support by using standardized procurement-assessment instruments. The Higher Education Community Vendor Assessment Toolkit (HECVAT) instrument from the Higher Education Information Security Council at EDUCAUSE is a risk assessment tool used in the procurement process to standardize the questions that colleges and universities might ask of technology vendors. Recently, EDUCAUSE unveiled new sections for the HECVAT instrument that are focused on the accessibility of the products and tools under review (see Shachmut 2021), making accessibility a core factor in determining which products colleges and universities purchase. In buying technology tools that are more accessible, we can set conditions that will later support both basic accessibility and UDL.

Perhaps the thorniest resource question around accessibility practices relates to the human resources we can bring to bear, especially if we aren't able to scale up the size of our staff rapidly in our academic- and student-support areas. I spoke with Rebecca Mushtare and Sean Moriarty at the State University of New York (SUNY) Oswego about their digital accessibility program. They shared how their leadership team was able to get people to include general accessibility in their everyday work. Rebecca notes that without leadership support, efforts to adopt accessibility methods are slow and spread only organically.

> Initially it was grassroots. There was no money when I first got here in 2012. I did a couple of workshops as part of our professional development series, like using screen readers and designing documents to be more accessible. Our instructional designer came to those workshops, and she and I connected. We started building more workshops and a work group and expanding who was part of it. We invited the library, our digital services team, marketing and communication people, IT, and obviously our disability-services people were looped in at the very beginning. And then we talked about how it was important to have faculty and students represented. That's how our accessibility-fellow program got started. (personal communication 21 Nov. 2023)

Sean continues by talking about one thing that magically allows money and hiring to flow: getting sued.

> So, we got the OCR [Office of Civil Rights] complaint about our website not being accessible. Our marketing and communication office got sued, but we rapidly brought in lots of other areas to address the complaint. With the president's office involved, there was a sense of urgency and importance. The deeper I got into it, the more I saw that if we don't build the right systems and support mechanisms, we'd fix it here and there, yes, but it's going to be whack-a-mole. There are too many people with their hands inside the website [to be able] to really resolve the problem. How were we going to train every secretary on campus who puts content on the website not to do things the way they used to?
>
> With the quantity of work that was being done, the only solution that I saw was hiring someone to help out. We prioritized it and put a staff resource towards it. Kate DeForest

> had been a student of Rebecca's, and I hired her as a graduate assistant. When she graduated, we hired her full time to work on remediation. Meanwhile, we redirected some of our staff to training efforts, so that we circled a date on the calendar and said, "we're doing accessible materials 100 percent as of this date," and we had staffed up to support that. It meant stretching out some other timelines, but when you have only so much time to show the government that you're making progress, it clarifies your priorities for you. (personal communication 23 Nov. 2023)

Now, you don't have to be sued to establish a resource profile to support the core accessibility work that your institution will do (S. Moriarty 2018). Ordinarily, though, we operate on thin margins, with little slack in terms of the resources we can allocate to any given effort. That's why the third part of making UDL possible has to do with how we prioritize our collective time.

Step 0.3 Making Time for UDL

Nearly every time I work with colleges and universities on UDL adoption, I hear some variation of "we don't have enough time to do this work thoroughly/well/at all." The perspective among many campus leaders is that, even if a framework like UDL promises smoother processes and reduced workload for learners, instructors, and staff, our institutions can't just pause every other part of our work to put in the effort on UDL. Likewise, UDL isn't the only framework competing for attention to address our various campus goals. It can be challenging to say "we will prioritize our UDL efforts" when we're also working on broad expansions of the diversity, number, and types of programs we offer. So, why—and how—should we set aside other efforts, even temporarily, to create space for everyone on campus to identify and work on an access-based element of their engagements with learners? We should define where we are already doing "extra" work, understand our collective capacities, determine who will do the work, and hold space for everyone to be involved, including our part-time and adjunct employees.

In our advice to individual higher-education practitioners about starting points for UDL work, Kirsten Behling and I advocate that people should look for the "pinch points" in the work that they do regularly, and

> identify the places within a given course where UDL strategies offer the greatest benefit for faculty members and learners. Most faculty members, if they have taught a course a few times, know where these pinch points are. In fact, they often engender watercooler stories that start with "can you believe that my students. . . ." Try this thought experiment. Call to mind a course, one that you have taught a few times or one for which you were part of the development team. Now, think of specific examples of the following criteria. Where do learners always
>
> - bring up the same questions every time the course is offered,
> - get things wrong on quizzes and tests, and
> - ask for alternate explanations? (Tobin and Behling 2018, 109)

When we think about scaling up our efforts, identifying the pinch points can help us to understand where we are already putting in repeated work that could be reduced, eliminated, or repurposed through a small amount of intentional design work.

For instance, I recently held a semester-long "UDL Champions" series of online seminars for colleagues at D'Youville University in

Buffalo, New York. Ashley Olsen, their Assistant Director of Accessibility and Tutoring Services, used her participation in the seminar to measure the repeated task work she was doing (see Olsen 2023). She discovered that she was spending more than seventy-five hours every semester emailing and following up with students who were eligible for, but did not yet request, disability accommodations that they had received in the past. Olsen often sent up to five reminder emails, with only a 60 percent open rate. When she adopted a plus-one approach to her communications (sending an email plus a text message to learners' mobile phone numbers), she saw the number of non-responders go from more than twenty per semester to zero; all students requested timely accommodations. Considering that the project of collecting data, adjusting the communication process, and tracking the results entailed about twenty-five hours of effort, it was well worth making time to save time. This has allowed Olsen to refocus her efforts away from follow-up communication and toward more intensive and direct engagement with her office's student clients.

To understand our collective capacity, and where we are engaged in repetitive efforts that could benefit from intentional design or redesign efforts, campus leaders can ask for formal work audits from each area of campus. A simpler way to collect meaningful data is to ask each frontline leader to collect a response to a single question: "where do you do repeated work to address the same issue, concern, or question?" Our employees know where the inefficiencies, redundancies, and circular processes are in the work they do for our learners. Whether it's bouncing students from office to office because no one is clearly responsible for responding to questions, or students asking the same question over and over about the directions for filling out a financial aid form, the initial stage of making time for UDL is to identify where we are already putting in repetitive work or work that attends to failed initial resolutions of concerns.

Once we know what access barriers and time sinks are present to our employees and learners, we can understand who needs to be involved to do the work itself. Starting with base accessibility needs allows us to create interdisciplinary and cross-functional groups and teams of colleagues: structures that will persist into later efforts to adopt UDL principles across the institution. Rather than ask individual employees to work alone to address barriers and repetitive work, our task as campus leaders is to group together similar challenges and give both responsibility and authority to our colleagues to call in resources to help them. This is why it is important first to establish accessible materials and instructional support resources: once we identify the big access gaps, it's time to call on those resources to address the gaps in a collaborative way.

How can we make time in what are already overloaded schedules among our employees? Especially for our part-time staff and adjunct faculty members, who are statistically most likely to be the first line of communication (Zhu 2021) with students who have questions or concerns about their studies. Three interconnected strategies help us to build capacity where we might not otherwise perceive we have it. Setting up these elements now also prepares our campus community for our main UDL efforts later on.

First, we assign accessibility work to every staff member in a small and open-ended way: ask every employee to choose an action to take within a given time frame. Second, we postpone or remove at least one expectation from everyone's work. This usually takes the form of asking frontline leaders to reprioritize the work their staff and instructors are doing. Last, we ask for a report of the effects of the small-scale accessibility change: how much effort or time was saved, over all?

An example of a program that "made time" for base accessibility is Goodwin University. I spoke recently with Diana LaRocco, their Dean of the School of Applied Liberal Arts and Social Sciences. She joined the university in 2016 expressly to help them to adopt UDL, with the support of the university president. LaRocco wrote and received a grant for Davis Foundation funding to provide time and job-embedded training across the entire institution:

> We did our best to apply all best practices of professional learning based on what we know. . . . You have to pay people to show up, give them course releases, or pay them, or let them know that this is important and should move to the front of the line in terms of expectations and outcomes. To this day, people get a $1,200 stipend for participating in Goodwin's training seminar, and they get a t-shirt, and they get a certificate. To me, the most important part is that we frame this as professional learning. It's not PD [professional development]; it's professional *learning*, and therefore worth a tangible reward in terms of time and effort. (personal communication 9 Sep. 2023)

Dawn Macaulay is the dean of innovative learning and Ranya Khan is the associate dean of teaching excellence at Humber University. I spoke with them about their UDL journey, and they both emphasized how creating the conditions to make UDL possible was the key to getting their efforts going in recent years. Macaulay shared that "we started in our strategic plan, in 2018 to talk about UDL as being part of our accessibility goals. Because we're a college system in Ontario, access was one of our early mandates—it was a requirement. We wanted to increase our accessibility to learners in our community."

Khan continued, "the unique thing was bringing together people from the accessibility services side of the house with the academic side of the house to work together on this: faculty members, academic support staff, and our center for teaching and learning." By establishing a conversation among the various siloes of campus around accessibility and accommodation, the campus was prepared for the next steps when their president set a goal of becoming the "most inclusive" campus in Ontario. This included adopting inclusive design frameworks and practices across the institution: a perfect fit for their later UDL efforts (Student Wellness & Accessibility Centre 2020)—about which you'll read more in later chapters.

Creating Conditions

Recently, I was invited to a university in the Midwestern United States to offer a keynote talk, workshop, and leadership consultation on UDL. During the leadership conversation, I sat down with the provost, registrar, and the heads of the academic affairs, student services, library, information technology, facilities, diversity, accessibility, academic advising, and public safety units. Our conversation began with questions about how their university could move from theory into practice at scale, with various stakeholders asking how best to support instructors to learn how to caption their own media, how to create accessible document formats, and otherwise craft accessible materials for their learners.

This approach is common among our campus leadership teams; we can jump directly from theories and frameworks into "how do we get our people doing the work?" This is a splendid question to ask, and also too soon in the UDL-at-scale process to ask it. Regardless of where your role sits in the institutional organizational chart, as a campus leader, your task is not to direct your colleagues to do the work, whatever work that might be.

Rather, our collective responsibility as leaders is to create the conditions under which our goals are possible to accomplish. Too often, we leap directly into "let's all get trained and take action" without first examining who can come to the training at all, and who further has space in their work processes to actually implement practices that contribute toward our shared goals.

In this chapter on creating the conditions for UDL to be possible, you've encountered three of the five core shifts that support a UDL-at-scale effort. Shift two is "individual applications give way to systemic practices." By understanding how widespread our fundamental accessibility efforts are currently, we can map where to direct scarce resources like funds and human capital. Where we cannot bring more resources to bear, we can at least change the time scale for action, slowing effort on other elements of our campus work to create space for accessibility to become a core effort across our service areas, as you saw in the example from Goodwin University. Shift three is "harnessing the power of defaults." By making accessibility a visible and expected part of the way we conduct our work, from procurement to design to operations, we can nudge people into following accessible design paths, as our colleagues did at SUNY Oswego. In shift four, "our efforts move beyond the classroom." By making accessibility a priority for service areas at California State University at Los Angeles, campus leaders signaled where resources should flow in response to needs that they assessed and measured.

A Call to Action

As you begin your UDL-at-scale efforts, set aside immediate actions in favor of first assessing capacity. Work with your colleagues in all areas of your organization to understand the state of the accessible content and materials you create and provide, measure staff capacity for supporting everyday accessibility practices, and determine how much time people are spending on their core work efforts—and how we observe and measure our own efforts to teach and support them. Once you have these data about the capacity for change at your institution, it's time to commit resources to support core accessibility processes.

A final thought about creating conditions for UDL: we need not wait until we have perfect accessibility practices before we continue the UDL-at-scale journey. Don't let the need for core accessibility data and resources stop the progress of your scaling-up efforts. Rather, once you have a better understanding about how your college or university is positioned to support accessibility, commit to strengthening those resources and move on to the next phase of the scaling-up process, in which you will codify your collective commitment through the establishment and evolution of policies and regular practices that acknowledge and create expectations for UDL done at scale.

4

PERMIT UDL

Policy and Practice

Once the conditions to make universal design for learning (UDL) are in place at your institution, the next step is one that many colleges and universities skip over in favor of beginning with pilot or small-scale efforts. Before you can engage in collective UDL efforts at scale, your institution needs to signal its support for the principles, methods, and goals of UDL itself. In chapter 3, we outlined how to make UDL possible through "base accessibility" workload analysis, support-capacity building, and cross-unit collaboration. Now, in this chapter, you will learn how to make UDL permitted at your institution. The word "permitted" might sound curious here, and I use it intentionally. In most hierarchical organizations, there is a well-developed (some might say overdeveloped) sense of what people are allowed to do within the policies and usual practices of the institution.

UDL, strictly speaking, is not a collection of individual teaching practices or decisions made in the moment by our instructors and staff members. Rather, the UDL framework guides the intentional design choices that we make *before* learners ever come to our service desks, classrooms, labs, and other spaces where they engage with us. UDL allows us to ask everyone in our organization to adhere to principles that lower access barriers in as many environments as possible. Because not everyone will adopt UDL principles on their own—due to a myriad of factors that we examined in chapter 2—creating permission to adopt and practice the UDL principles is a necessary stage in a scaled-up adoption process. It's also the stage of the scaling-up process that takes the longest amount of time on most campuses, so it's important to work on this part of your UDL-at-scale project early and run it in parallel with later stages.

Because the UDL framework is a means toward strengthening our systems, it's unlikely that adding it to our policy manual or workflow processes will, by itself, lead to changed actions among our employees. A quick thought experiment will serve to illustrate this point. Think of a policy or goal at your school, college, or university that you have seen, but it doesn't have an effect directly on your day-to-day work. For instance, at the University of Wisconsin–Madison, where I used to work, there is a policy that states that everyone on campus "must make reasonable efforts to . . . minimize . . . foot traffic on turf" (UW–Madison 2003). In other words, walk only on the paved surfaces of campus. The desire paths worn into the various lawns across campus testify to how poorly known and followed this policy is. No individual at our institutions can know or follow the entirety of our policy manuals, which are typically huge documents. If you were to print your policy manual, it might hurt if you dropped it on your foot.

So, why, if people won't or can't remember specific policies, is it important to engage in policy creation to support our campus-wide UDL efforts? In their day-to-day work, everyone has so many "must do" tasks and parameters to remember that campus leaders need to break through the thicket of policies to create a clear, simple, imperative for UDL. Paradoxically, having UDL "on the books" is a foundation for arguing that inclusive designs and practices should be part of our everyday work list of "must do" items.

In other words, we can't ask all our employees to adopt UDL principles if they aren't yet part of our shared expectations. In this chapter, you'll learn strategies for incorporating UDL into policy in ways that lead to action and support, and you'll encounter people who have been successful in bringing UDL into the policy landscape at their schools.

Policy: Look to the EAST

As we begin to build processes for adopting UDL across entire institutions, we should discuss a paradox. The UDL framework explicitly offers many ways to accomplish the three principles of multiple means of engagement, representation, and action/expression—these are the thirty-six considerations within the UDL framework. In many instances, however, practitioners use these considerations as prescriptive checklists. Do these specific things, and voilà: UDL. Mary Quirke, Conor McGuckin, and Patricia McCarthy outline this paradox succinctly in their book *Adopting a UDL Attitude within Academia*:

> Implementing UDL as a simple hands-on toolkit underestimates the power of the approach. . . . All too often we have heard colleagues declare that they have used the model and "UDL'd" something—for example, changed a module assessment. . . . The danger is that any UDL approach will become a checklist or template approach to what we do. (2024, 47).

As we shift from framing UDL for individuals in higher education to acting at scale, it can be tempting to create policy and practices that ask everyone in the institution to take exactly the same actions and create templates for behavior that will satisfy the UDL principles in their design and implementation. The UDL framework itself doesn't specify the "how" for implementing any of the thirty-six considerations, even though each consideration is supported by possible examples (see CAST's *UDL Guidelines* website for the details).

As you've seen in the previous chapters, scaling up our UDL efforts requires us to create simpler, more easily achieved goals that everyone in our organizations can accomplish. We should also explicitly call for creativity and provide freedom to work within the boundaries of the UDL framework—allow and encourage our employees to dive deep into the thirty-six considerations and select methods that align best with the work that they do for our learners.

A formal policy-development approach can help us to keep our focus on outcomes rather than methods when we include UDL in the policies of our organizations. The success of a UDL-at-scale initiative is measured in the breadth of behavioral change across the everyday efforts of everyone in our institutions. The Behavioural Insights Team in the Australian government coined the EAST framework (Service et al. 2014) as a mnemonic aid to creating policy from a behavioral approach: stating and supporting the behaviors that we wish to see happen. The letters in the EAST acronym ask us to make desired behaviors—in this case, adopting UDL principles and practices—easy, attractive, social, and timely.

Easy. Adopt policies that reduce the "hassle factor" of taking up an action. By reducing the effort required to take action, we increase buy-in and adoption. For example, you saw in chapter 3 how accessible-materials development at California State University at Los Angeles had been sporadic until the establishment of an Accessible Instructional Materials (AIM) process. To make this practice a permitted reality, the university system adopted a formal policy that made accessible materials the responsibility of the entire system, and defined accessible-materials creation as a service provided to learners and instructors, rather than a responsibility of learners and instructors to seek out (California State University 2013).

Attractive. Making our UDL-at-scale initiatives personally meaningful or rewarding for everyone in the college or university is a second element we can include in policy statements. Greensboro College made a policy-based commitment to become "a universal design for learning (UDL) institution" (Bogdan 2018). This includes a UDL goal as one of the four pillars in their five-year strategic plan (Greensboro College 2022), with incentives for all staff and instructors to lower barriers to learning in all learner engagements. This reduces the individual effort needed to "do" UDL well: as the campus adopts UDL principles, each employee needs to do comparatively less to contribute. See the "UDL Policies" callout box for more about Greensboro College.

Social. The establishment of communities and networks to support key efforts in the institution can be enshrined in policy that asks for such communities to be established and to report or share on their outputs on a regular basis as part of the shared governance of the institution. For example, Boston College established a UDL task force in 2013 as part of its updates to existing accessibility policy (Boston College 2024).

Timely. Because "behavior is generally easier to change when habits are already disrupted," a policy priority for UDL at scale is to ask for regularly repeating checks on the state of UDL efforts. "Prompt people to identify the barriers to action and develop a specific plan to address them" (Service et al. 2014) as part of the regular review of efforts at the college or university to respond to accreditation renewal, for example.

Each of the elements in the EAST framework allows our institutional policies to move beyond statements of ideals into ways of defining what an effectively functioning inclusively designed campus should look like. In adding to or modifying our existing policies, we move beyond performative inclusion—saying that we value doing the right thing—into active inclusion—creating policies that will later support structures, norms, and practices at the institutional level. Taken together, new policies and practices shift our collective expectations, measurements, rewards, and consequences around inclusive work.

By including UDL intentionally in the policy landscape of our institutions, UDL becomes not a response to one concern, but to the gestalt needs of campus. Today, most colleges and universities have ideal endpoint policies that outline broad goals of inclusive teaching and practices, yet very few of us actually implement inclusive practices of any kind, let alone specialized sets of principles like UDL. This is why we must pair our policy development with practice-based efforts to make UDL a part of our everyday work.

Practice: Move FAST

In terms of establishing everyday practices and expectations for our UDL-at-scale efforts, the FAST framework (Sull and Sull 2018) from the MIT Sloan School of Management allows us to shift from individual expectations to an at-scale set of collective targets:

> According to conventional wisdom, goals should be specific, measurable, achievable, realistic, and time-bound. But SMART goals undervalue ambition, focus narrowly on individual performance, and ignore the importance of discussing goals throughout the year. To drive strategy execution,

> leaders should instead set goals that are FAST—frequently discussed, ambitious, specific, and transparent. (Sull and Sull 2018)

Frequently discussed. This is the piece of campus-wide cultural changes that is often overlooked. Planning for frequent and prominent check-ins increases the odds of success for any campus-level change. Keeping the goal in front of all campus staff through reiteration, check-ins, and reporting creates two benefits. It coalesces a sense of shared endeavor and identity among the various ordinarily siloed units of our colleges and universities, and creates channels for feedback and shared-action planning. Jenn Wicks is the director of the Center for Teaching and Learning Innovation at the College of the North Atlantic in Newfoundland, Canada. When I spoke to her about her campus efforts to adopt UDL, she recounted how their campus leadership wanted to create a new teacher certification program. They used its development as a vehicle for bringing UDL principles into everyone's daily practices. Through the development of a UDL unit in a teacher-training micro-course and the embedding of UDL principles and practices throughout, the three principles, nine guidelines, and thirty-six considerations of UDL are consistently part of every conversation about good teaching at the college (personal communication, June 24, 2024).

Ambitious. The goal of adopting UDL principles across an entire college or university is by its very nature a large and complex endeavor. Campus leaders who want to adopt UDL can use the complex nature of the challenge itself as a way to recognize and reward the skills distributed among our employees. By framing our UDL-at-scale goals in terms of "we can do this," our end goal shifts our work away from repetitive and reactive firefighting so that we can collectively apply our expertise to more entangled and challenging needs. One specific shift is "deliberately [to] decouple goal attainment from performance reviews and compensation decisions, which may seem like heresy to managers steeped in traditional performance management philosophy. But it's consistent with research that shows financial rewards are not the only way to boost performance of an individual or team. Indeed, specific, ambitious goals . . . spur performance on their own, without the need for financial incentives" (Sull and Sull 2018).

A UDL-at-scale example is Aurora University in Illinois, where Donna Liljegren is the dean of online and graduate studies, and Brianne DiPasquantonio is the assistant dean of online faculty recruitment and development. When the university brought in a new president and switched to a new learning management system (LMS) in a three-year span, people felt general license to examine and evaluate existing tools, methods, and practices. Across all support units of the university, an internal audit of practices identified repeated and reactive work being done because of access barriers for learners. As of this writing, Aurora University is in the process of adopting UDL across its course-development processes, as well as updating its instructional- design and media-services workflows (personal communication, July 26, 2024). This aligns with setting a UDL-at-scale goal to "minimize the risk that employees will sandbag by committing to overly conservative goals they are sure to achieve" (Sull and Sull 2018), by asking everyone to work toward ambitious UDL goals that are not tied to their promotion or raises, but to the overall success measures of the institution, such as continued accreditation.

Specific. Metrics and milestones are business terms that can sometimes feel foreign to the working conditions in higher education. How often have you heard feedback like "we don't turn out repeatably consistent widgets when we teach students" when implementing a quantifiable change to workflows or campus processes? The key to adopting specific goals for UDL at scale is that the control over outcomes should lie with our employees themselves. Instead of assigning performance or action targets to our staff and instructors, "employees translate their goals into clearly defined tasks and concrete measures of progress" (Sull and Sull 2018), for which supervisors then hold them accountable. To ensure that everyone creates UDL goals and ways to measure their individual progress, it is imperative that UDL be an explicit part of the standard job descriptions throughout the organization. Work with your faculty senate and/or campus unions to craft job-description language that puts UDL practices as required knowledge and responsibilities for all roles on campus. This is also a "secret sauce" for establishing UDL expectations that we will revisit at the end of the book, so remember "UDL in job descriptions" as a key piece of both the beginning and the end of the scaling-up process.

Transparent. Most goals for instructors and staff members at colleges and universities are tied directly to their individual promotions and salary increases. As you've seen above, this can create a perverse incentive to "sandbag," or set low-effort action goals that are easily achieved. In addition to decoupling action goals for UDL efforts from the employment-progression system, another way to make a campus-wide cultural shift visible is to share individual, department, and institutional goals in a public way. For instance, most colleges and universities share their top-level goals on an "about us" web page, and some departments and units do, as well. Extend this to every employee. On their individual contact pages within the online campus directory, ask them to list their yearly goals around key campus initiatives, including adoption, implementation, and maintenance of UDL principles. "Making goals public can boost performance by introducing peer pressure, showing employees what level of performance is possible, and helping them locate colleagues in similar situations who can provide advice on how they can do better" (Sull and Sull 2018).

UDL Policies: Greensboro College

Greensboro College in North Carolina crafted their recent five-year strategic plan with UDL as one of four foundational pillars for the plan. In response to the access needs made plain by the societal lockdowns of the COVID-19 global pandemic, when the time came in 2021 to draft their next five-year plan, learner agency and access were front-of-mind issues for Greensboro College's leaders. Building on the core accessibility services and practices that the college had implemented as a result of the pandemic, the new strategic plan explicitly calls upon UDL principles to underpin all aspects of the operations of the college:

> The four pillars upon which the college's strategic plan is founded:
>
> 1. A liberal-arts college
> 2. Faith formation
> 3. Community
> 4. A universal design for learning environment at the institutional level. (Greensboro College 2022)

Greensboro College has adopted UDL principles across all aspects of its operations: "content, context, and instruction benefit individual learning differences, to remove barriers so all students can be successful" due to the implementation of UDL "at the institutional level, including all academic, student development, campus infrastructure, and resource programs and units. UDL is the vocabulary, architecture, and framework for successful academic and student development for GC" (Greensboro College 2022).

Two common responses to mandates for inclusive action on behalf of employees at colleges and universities have to do with current resources and expectations. I often hear responses like "we don't have enough people to do all of that work—and, besides, no one has complained about not doing it, so far." Greensboro College's inclusion of UDL in its strategic plan is a step toward expanding the *identity* of the institution, so that those "no people, no time, no resources, and no urgency" concerns are beside the point, shifting UDL from "nice to do" to "mission critical." One of the three strategic priorities in their five-year plan at Greensboro College is access:

> **ACCESS** – Greensboro College will strengthen our campus community by fostering a healthier, more diverse and inclusive culture at all levels and in all areas. We will strive to decrease the financial burdens of our students by increasing financial support. Greensboro College wants to remain competitive as we seek the best fit students who will thrive and persist to graduation.
>
> - **Enhance Inclusion.** Offer opportunities and resources for equal access through programs such as UDL, DEI [diversity, equity, and inclusion], faith formation, student engagement and physical access.
> - **Expand Affordability.** Increase affordability through a multi-pronged approach including such initiatives as strategic tuition pricing and use of financial aid, increasing scholarship funding, and expand use of cost-effective materials and resources.

- **Strengthen Communication.** Improve information flow across internal and external constituencies. (Greensboro College 2022)

Greensboro College's director of academic accessibility, Georgieann Bogdan, points to UDL's inclusion in the strategic plan as the formal signal that now permits all areas within the college to perform the work of lowering access barriers. UDL

> empowers students to have a voice and makes them feel like they are important and responsible for a bright future. [It] focuses on the process, not just the outcome; builds in time to reflect and grow; leverages technology in meaningful ways; engages learners on multiple levels, accommodating many types of learners in a single classroom who thrive in different ways; [and] supports employees to try new things. Innovation can happen only if educators feel supported rather than just evaluated. (Bogdan 2018)

A Call to Action

To set the stage for UDL-at-scale actions, our campuses need to create conditions of "core accessibility" where UDL is possible and then set UDL explicitly into the policies and practices of the organization. By using the EAST and FAST frameworks, campus leaders create first-action signals to the rest of campus that not only is UDL a good idea, but that it is part of the collective identity and journey that we map out for our work together. As you examine your current policy and practice landscape, look for opportunities to

- reduce the "hassle factor" of taking desired actions,
- create a narrative of "taking work off our plates,"
- start or expand regular and frequent ways to talk together about UDL, and
- time major UDL efforts to coincide with or support other big changes.

Create spaces for frequent conversations about individual goals that support institutional UDL goals by decoupling them from employment evaluations, giving employees control over their own expression of UDL goals, and encouraging transparency through the accountability of public sharing to create good peer pressure and keep the conversation about UDL going across campus.

Once you have policies and desired practices in place, it becomes easier to begin the collective work. While you need not wait until all your policies reflect or contain UDL to begin to execute your UDL-at-scale vision, having key policy drivers in place will make the journey of adoption smoother. In the next chapter, you'll discover specific actions to take to support UDL changes for your campus community.

5

SUPPORT UDL

Getting to Scale

You've established the conditions under which universal design for learning (UDL) can happen. You've signaled your institutional commitment to lowering access barriers across all of the engagements that learners have with your employees, instructors, and support units. Now it's time for the actual execution of your plans to implement UDL across campus, at scale. What does success look like in this phase of campus-wide UDL adoption? The eventual goal is to transform what can seem like the "extra" effort of applying the UDL framework to our various design work and interactions into an expected part of our everyday work. For the implementation phase of the UDL-at-scale process, the milestones toward which you're aiming are now smaller: making space and time for UDL efforts to happen at all, creating clear and achievable measurements for progress, and co-creating action plans to guide the work that the project entails.

In this chapter, you'll learn how to actually do the work of scaling up UDL efforts, using the stories of people and institutions whose UDL journeys are good models for the rest of us, and framing the process through an established (and perhaps already familiar) project-management model. The support phase of scaling up UDL takes a long time. Most campus-wide UDL adoption projects work on the scale of years—from a single year for projects that build on robust existing foundations in comparatively small colleges or universities all the way up to four to six years for projects where UDL is entirely new to large, complex organizations. Going from scattered, voluntary, individual UDL efforts to whole-campus adoption requires a systemic yet flexible approach, allowing everyone in the organization to aim for the same goals while defining the actual work to be done at the local level.

Creating, managing, and tracking UDL projects for your entire institution are all made easier by following the formal process-based stages of project management as laid out by the Project Management Institute (PMI 2021): initiating, planning, executing, monitoring, and closing. While you don't need to be a formal project manager yourself, it's good practice to enlist the help of the people in your organization with project management experience, whether you have a formal project management office (PMO) or you can lean on expertise among your colleagues on the staff or faculty. The five-step process outlined here has echoes of the CAST UDL implementation process of "explore, prepare, integrate, scale, and optimize" (Rose, Ralabate and Meo 2010; Meo and Currie-Rubin 2015); as well as Eric Moore's "pre-implementation, individual, community, unit, and institution" progression (Moore et al. 2018); and Loui Lord Nelson and James Basham's *Blueprint for UDL* that follows an "explore, prepare, launch, sustain" (2014, 9) cycle.

Support Phase 1: Initiating UDL at Scale

The most successful large-scale projects are those where change comes about in response to patterns of evidence. You can use UDL's focus on addressing access barriers in a practical way to get everyone in your college or university on board. Think about the ways that people in your college or university perceive and communicate change. You have likely seen ambitious projects on your campus that fizzled out because not everyone saw the need to act. Such projects can be perceived as adopting new things for the sake of novelty alone or changing practices in the name of efficiency or cost savings. Neither of these are powerful motivators for large-scale changes (see Breckenridge, et al. 2019). Rather, we should frame UDL at scale as a way to touch on intrinsic motivations and find arguments that resonate across campus stakeholder groups.

In the first phase of a formal project, leaders formally authorize the project by creating a charter: a document that collects initial requirements and addresses the needs and expectations of the various stakeholders in the institution. The development of a UDL project charter requires insight into and data collection about the resources that are available to your institution. This is groundwork that supports how you will assign time, funds, and people to do the work of your UDL implementation, and it helps to define the level to which you will be able to monitor and capture the results of the work that will take place. For a UDL campus-wide adoption, a project charter should include five elements: the business case, a proposed contract that outlines actions, a review of environmental factors, a list of organizational assets, and a stakeholder analysis.

1.1: The UDL Business Case

A business case is a narrative that provides information about how the results of performing the project are worth the investment of resources. For UDL implementations, business cases are often built around market demand (in the form of greater enrollments at institutions with lower access barriers), organizational need (access as a stated goal in the institutional mission, vision, or values), social need (using UDL as a supporting frame for diversity, equity, inclusion, and access goals), or some combination of these. Further, a UDL business case formally outlines the partnership between the requesters and those who will perform the work, and it assigns authority to those who will apply resources to the project's tasks.

In your institution, connect with colleagues who regularly track aggregate data about learners. Operational Data Store (ODS) or information technology teams often work in concert with the registrar, financial-aid, counseling, and other support areas across campus to track learner persistence, retention, and satisfaction. Collect information about gaps or areas of potential where learners engage with your institution in various ways. Consider not only how learners fare once they are in classroom environments, but take into account their journey to the classroom. How many learning situations must they master before they ever take courses? For instance, examine data about how many people apply to be students at your institution but who do not enroll. Track how many people are accepted to your college or university but do not register for courses (or register for too few, too many, or not in time). Data like these can indicate access gaps, which should drive the formation of the business case for UDL.

An example of a UDL business case comes to us from Ash Mitchell, Julia Larsen, and Grace Troup from the instructional design team at the University of Nebraska–Lincoln. When I spoke with them recently, they shared how an accessibility audit led to large-scale buy-in for UDL across the entire campus. During the COVID-19 pandemic, UN–Lincoln instructors, like their counterparts worldwide, had to adapt quickly to emergency remote instruction. Likewise, student-service offices also had to pivot to remote support work. During 2020 and 2021, the instructional design team promoted accessible design and UDL as ways to lower barriers not only for students, but also to make emergency remote teaching smoother and more effective for instructors.

After a colleague performed a general accessibility audit on learning- management-system (LMS) course environments, the UN–Lincoln instructional designers created a how-to resource about effective teaching practices. This resource was developed in collaboration with many other campus units: disability-support, institutional equity, compliance, information technology, libraries, and diversity & inclusion. The developers crafted a business case narrative to present the training module to their Academic Solutions Council, composed of all the associate deans across the institution. The developers hoped to obtain buy-in from a few associate deans to do a pilot program; instead, all members of the Academic Solutions Council signed on, and the team began working up to scale.

1.2: The Proposed Contract

As you saw in the previous chapter, an at-scale UDL adoption will engage everyone in the institution with broader goals, while allowing individual latitude to define how specifically to meet those goals. In your UDL project charter, create a proposed contract: a prediction about what types of support the institution will offer to help everyone to reach the shared goals of the project. It can also include the criteria for judging whether the work that is produced actually does lower access barriers for learners and/or fosters greater learner agency. This element of the initial charter will evolve over time, so the initial aim is not to be comprehensive or final with the contract elements, but to define at a high level what resources will be committed to the overall effort in terms of people, time, and funds.

A further element of the proposed contract is to specify who does the work of the implementation project. As I've discussed above, part of the challenge of UDL adoption in higher education is that it currently falls disproportionately on the shoulders of instructors (King-Sears, et al. 2023). In the contract for campus-wide UDL implementation, specify what roles key stakeholders will play, including instructor-facing areas such as media services, information technology, and unit chairs, along with student-facing service areas like the library, registrar, academic counseling, tutoring, and mental-health support teams. We will expand on who to include in this list in the *Stakeholder Analysis* section below.

As a good example of a project-charter contract, Diana LaRocco spoke with me about how Goodwin University became a UDL institution. LaRocco identified many background conditions that made UDL a fruitful topic for exploration, such as teacher-partnership grant funding in the early 2010s, a Davis Foundation grant to study UDL in 2016, and the first cohort of on-the-job staff trainings that included UDL in 2017. She also identified the key drivers that were part of the proposed contract between the administration of the university and its instructors and staff members. Leadership committed to supporting the UDL effort in terms of staff time and funding to create cultural change as well as policy-based change. The elements of the UDL project at Goodwin fit well with their mission "to educate a diverse student population in a dynamic environment that aligns education, commerce, and community" (Goodwin University 2015). LaRocco added that the proposed contract from the early stages of their UDL adoption project has remained as a continued commitment and road map, helping them in their continued expansion of the project as they measure and assess the impact of their efforts.

1.3: Environmental Factors

The project charter for your UDL implementation should also include a description of your campus climate and culture, what project managers call "environmental factors." These include the types of information typically found in institutional datasets:

resources available to the project; types of technology and tools in common use; the number, types, and level of programs and curricula; broad patterns of characteristics of your learner populations; and the existence of previous work that could serve as starting points or foundations for your UDL project.

Each of these environmental factors should have a narrative related to how it can support, pose a barrier to, or shape the overall project of adopting UDL principles across campus. For instance, Darla Kearney, the UDL teaching and learning consultant at Mohawk College, shared with me that her institution adopted UDL because of three environmental factors. First, the enacting of the Accessibility for Ontarians with Disabilities Act, or AODA (Government of Ontario 2005), created a legal landscape that required the college (along with every company and organization receiving provincial funds) to address access barriers in a systemic fashion. Further, the administration of the college had adopted UDL into its policy manuals and progress indicators, and instructors were asking "who will help us with this?" Finally, the college had adopted a Teaching for Success initiative to train every instructor—including, and especially, part-time instructors—in evidence-based teaching practices, among which was UDL. All of these environmental factors went into a project charter to perform research about identifying and addressing gaps and challenges to learner retention. This eventually became a grant application, a research protocol, and an open-access book entitled *Universal Design for Learning (UDL) for Inclusion, Diversity, Equity, and Accessibility (IDEA)* (Kearney 2022). All of these results stemmed from a comprehensive and detailed project charter.

1.4: Organizational Assets

In addition to the list of environmental factors, your UDL project charter should contain a list of assets that your college or university can reasonably provide to support and do the work of the project. This section of the charter should address the resource "iron triangle" of people, time, and funds available, as well as affordances such as software, physical space, and partnerships with external entities.

Your institution's project-management officers or business team are experienced in estimating resources needed for large-scale efforts, and you can do some rough outlining using techniques such as expert judgment (asking people who have done similar work to share how long and how many resources they required), analogous estimation (going back to previous projects undertaken by your institution to uncover patterns of how large projects ordinarily unfold), or parametric estimation (starting with what one person can do and multiplying to get a rough guess about effort and resources). For the charter, it's not necessary, and might even be counterproductive, to get too specific about how you will use your asset list (see the section on "Planning" below for more about that process). Rather, this is the place to enumerate as complete a list as possible of all the financial, human, time, and tool resources that you can apply to the project. This gives you a better understanding of the maximum scope of the project and allows you to make early adjustments.

For instance, when I spoke with Anna Greene, Carrie Hansel, Michael Mace, and Caitlin Malone on the Indiana University digital-accessibility team, they talked about the importance of identifying what products and tools in common use on campus were themselves possible barriers to a larger mission of creating accessible learning interactions for students. Mace talked about "stopping inaccessible products at the gate" as a step toward understanding what they could collectively do with the people, time, tools, and funds they had available. Once they had a clearer census of which departments had licenses for which tools (in addition to the campus-wide tool sets supported by their central information technology team), they were better able to create a charter with clear goals, actions to take, and benefits for the campus.

1.5: Stakeholder Analysis

Beyond simply naming the stakeholder groups who will take part in or be affected by your proposed UDL project, a key final element in the project charter is to situate the various stakeholder groups along vectors of their interest, involvement, and impact on the project's possible success. A stakeholder analysis for the project charter should also go beyond the "usual" stakeholder groups. Think beyond the institution itself and create a stakeholder context diagram (see Smith 2000). For every phase of the project, consider who will likely

- direct and approve the work,
- perform the tasks of the project,
- need to stay informed about project progress,
- be affected by the project's outputs,
- need to make changes based on the project's effects, and
- become interested in the project, even if they were not part of the initial stakeholder group.

The "invisible" stakeholders who are not ordinarily part of the workforce or directly affected by the work are perhaps the most important ones to discover and include in your initial analysis. These are people and groups like legislators, the media, your institution's peers/competitors, product vendors, and even campus groups like the facilities and grounds teams. Think of people and teams who don't ordinarily have a say in the direction of major projects, but whose work nonetheless changes when projects are implemented. Proactively acknowledging voices that could support or derail project work is the key to the charter list and analysis of stakeholder groups.

A good example of stakeholder analysis for a UDL campus-wide adoption is from Elinor Olausson, Ann Heelan, and Kjetil Knarlag. In their chapter of the book *Transforming Higher Education through UDL: An International Perspective* (2019), they describe the Universal Design for Learning: License to Learn (UDLL) project in Norway. Their team used an appreciative-inquiry approach to identify and engage with four key stakeholder groups: students, instructors, administrators, and disability-support offices. The authors began with students to keep their needs and characteristics as drivers for their project. Instructors were analyzed according to their cultural and logistical openness to effecting positive change in their work. Administrators were polled about their major goals: un-silo-ing of efforts across institutions and better measurable markers of learner success and progress. Disability-support leaders were selected as a key stakeholder group because of their long-standing advocacy for lowering barriers, as well as their desire to use UDL to lower general barriers so that their staff could focus more of their efforts on learners who need more intensive affordances and support. These four groups are likely not the only ones, or perhaps even the right ones, for your institutional scenario, so it is important before beginning a UDL adoption at scale to understand who will guide, work on, and be informed about the progress of the work.

Initiating Process Summary

To sum up, in the project charter for your UDL-at-scale adoption project, identify who will lead the UDL campus work, and go beyond just support from leaders. Create expectations from them for the people who will actually perform the tasks of implementation. Make a business case for the urgent need to integrate the social model of disability—where barriers exist in the environment rather than inherently in people—into teaching and learning. Craft a model contract that outlines the benefits of engaging in the work of the project, both from a social-justice and sustainable-practice perspective, as well as through a budgetary lens—is it worth it to engage in adopting UDL at scale? Scan the environment for people and groups who can support or hinder the progress of the UDL project. Gather information about the resources that you can apply to the project, and be realistic about the funds, time, people, and tools in your portfolio. And acknowledge the changing demographics among our learners and employees through stakeholder analysis.

All the preparatory work described so far has been part of the process of initiating your project: this is the work that you do to determine whether the at-scale implementation project is even viable yet. Perhaps in creating your charter, you discover you have enough people, time, and tools, but lack the funding to properly engage. This would be a clear sign to work with your grants team to identify sources of financial support. The end goal of this first phase of your UDL project is to come up with a general description of your project and a decision about its feasibility (or a rewritten project that has a different scope or use of resources that falls within your boundaries).

Support Phase 2: Planning UDL at Scale

Once you have created a project charter, it's time to start the planning process. The information in your UDL project charter should provide you with a clear understanding of the resources that your college or university can apply to a UDL implementation. Now, creating the project plan allows you to assign resources along a timeline and recognize how various resources interact with and depend on one another. The core elements of a UDL-at-scale project plan outline the scope, activities, schedule, costs, communications, and risk analysis for the project.

2.1: Project Scope Planning

The scope of campus-wide efforts may seem obvious, but it's important to state the requirements of your UDL-at-scale project, both overall and in a format where the work to be done across campus is broken down by the various teams and individuals who will do the work. A good example of a scope statement that shares requirements and creates a work breakdown structure (WBS) is the collection of documents that established Landmark College in Vermont. Landmark College expressly serves students with learning differences, and its charter documents established, from its inception in the early 1980s, that the new institution would aim to reduce student-to-instructor ratios; "become increasingly recognized as the center of excellence for teaching, research, and training in the learning disabilities field;" and create a research institute to study learning differences (MacGuire 2023).

A key part of a UDL-at-scale plan is what project managers call a "premortem" analysis. In medicine a postmortem, or after-death, examination helps coroners determine how people died. The practitioner carefully examines and probes the body to see what caused damage and failure. In large projects, premortem analyses are much less grim, but equally purposeful. Connect with the stakeholders whom you identified in the Initiating phase of your UDL project and ask them to imagine that the project has just concluded, and to identify what challenges or barriers led to its success or failure. For instance, ask colleagues to identify, define, and narrate their "pinch points": current problem areas, processes, and interactions that repeatedly don't go as planned. Then ask them to predict why efforts to address those pinch points did or didn't work out. By putting stakeholders across campus into the mindset of helping to explore how and why proposed efforts will or won't be effective, we subtly shift their thinking and sense of agency in the overall process. Stakeholders should see UDL as a response to pressures they are themselves feeling and are as-yet unable to solve.

Performing a premortem exercise allows you to engage in the next step of the planning phase: defining the activities within the project. Rather than assigning task-level actions from a central authority, it's often smoother and more effective to convene a group of supervisors with responsibility over your organization's service areas (you likely already have such meetings regularly booked for other purposes), and ask them to engage their direct reports to come up with actions to take that will help them to meet the goals of the scale-up project. An important degree of freedom for your mid-level leaders is to determine what they can delay, reassign, or remove all together from the workload of their employees to focus on UDL efforts.

2.2: Activity Planning

Once you have outlined the scope and work activities in your plan, the next step is to define, sequence, and assign resources to the activities to achieve the project goals. In your activity plan, first define the types of tasks people will do, both to establish new processes and then to maintain things. A side note: it's not necessary to specify the actual work, here, just the types of activities. Leave room for local control and cocreation. For instance, instead of saying that the library will revise their bibliographic-instruction training modules to provide multiple means of action and expression for participants (too prescriptive), put an activity element into your campus plan for the library to identify the engagement most used by students and apply UDL principles to its design and facilitation. By identifying categories of work, you can more easily estimate (a) the sequence in which activities will need to happen, (b) what resources might be needed for each activity (people, funds, and materials), and (c) how much time each activity is likely to take.

2.3: Schedule Planning

Next, craft a project schedule. Note which activities can happen in parallel and which are dependent on others, adding a percentage of time for "slack" between and among the various activities to allow for variability in the schedule. A good example of a UDL project schedule is from Cindy Berhtram, Paloma Gutierrez, and Annie Sadler at Stanford University, who created an activity plan for their university's three-year Equity and Inclusion project and shared it on a website along with templates for others to use in creating their own higher-education project plans (see Berhtram, Gutierrez, and Sadler 2024).

2.4: Cost Planning

After planning the activities and schedule for your UDL project, estimate the costs associated with those efforts. Remember to include not only direct costs (things like materials and tools) but indirect costs (like the time and benefits needed to employ the people who are doing the work). In this part of the planning process, also create a quality plan and human-resources plan. List the baseline goals for success for each activity, and create a collective list of all the people who will need to perform activities in the various phases of the project. All these elements fall under "costs" because you and your leadership team will need to measure the outputs of the various activities. Were they successful, and did they require fewer or more resources than planned? For a model plan document that lists costs and quality markers for progress in a UDL implementation, refer to the Fitchburgh State University School of Business annual report (2022), in which the action plan, costs, and human-resource plans for the academic year are tied explicitly to the mission and goals of the school, requirements from accrediting bodies, and an explicit mandate "to develop instructional strategies that follow the principles of UDL and support student learning . . . that cultivates a culturally responsive environment" (Fitchburgh State University 2022).

2.5: Communication Planning

The next planning element for UDL at scale is to determine how you wish to communicate throughout and about the process. Plan in two different ways: create gradual concrete steps that everyone can follow so they feel supported in adopting UDL as part of their everyday work, and anticipate possible pushback or concerns by listening to stakeholder groups as you plan.

A good example of a UDL-adoption communication campaign comes from a master class that Frederic Fovet offered recently to the Australian Disability Clearinghouse on Education and Training (ADCET). Fovet argues that in trying to convince our organizational stakeholders of the benefits of UDL, we risk sabotaging our own efforts if we focus on the outputs rather than on practical actions to scale up our implementations. Fovet's communication strategy emphasizes flexibility, multiplicity of messaging, and tailoring of messages to stakeholder groups:

> **Avoid rigid delineations in your approaches to UDL.** Many stakeholders may have a UDL approach but not use that terminology; they must be invited in. UDL is not the only pedagogical philosophy that matters: constructivist, socio-constructivist, experiential, and critical pedagogies are equally important (but they may not be fully inclusive or

> accessible). . . . [Communications must] seek that "happy place" where good pedagogy and accessibility overlap. . . . [T]he way UDL is being presented to a campus . . . requires a literal process of branding, and much reflection around campus-wide strategy.
>
> **Find leverage.** There are multiple stakeholders on our campuses (faculty, student affairs and student services personnel, senior administration, etc.). Not all of these stakeholders will have the same interest in UDL. Find arguments that appeal to the full spectrum of interested parties. [At my institution, these] arguments were developed and grew as a result of constant triangulation following UDL workshops and intros. [They] eventually represented the concerns of all stakeholders encountered on campus. [There is no] "perfect" range of arguments. . . . [N]uance must be used when formulating a pitch.
>
> **Recognize and acknowledge a need.** Never rush into "selling" UDL to campus stakeholders. Instead, take the time to allow stakeholders to acknowledge what is not working in current processes related to inclusion and accessibility. [N]ot rushing [communications] allows participants to feel empowered by their own desire to seek solutions. Buy-in is much more likely to emerge if stakeholders can see UDL as a response to a pressure they are themselves feeling and are unable to solve. It is important to position UDL in relation to an existing need on your campus. Buy-in is dependent on your ability to lead stakeholders to see UDL as a response to a pressing need. These needs vary across campus and must all be acknowledged. (Fovet 2021)

As you plan your communication campaign, it can be tempting to approach various groups in your organization with a metaphorical tray of UDL tools and techniques: "here is something new that you can use in lots of ways!" That "selling" approach, as Fovet explains above, risks triggering pushback against novelty for its own sake. We're all aware of the "innovation fatigue" that sets in after people are with an organization long enough to see trends come and go over many years.

Rather, Fovet's communication plan meshes well with my own "pinch points" approach you encountered in chapter 3, where we listen to colleagues about what is already not going as planned in their everyday work. By focusing on where everyone is already willing to put in some effort to address issues that they themselves have defined, we position UDL as one tool in a toolkit for positive change.

2.6: Risk-Analysis Planning

The final step in the planning phase of your UDL-scaling project is risk assessment. Most of us think of risk only in its negative aspect: if we do this, then we risk that going wrong. Risk has both negative and positive valence, meaning that in addition to anticipating what could go differently than we plan for our campus-wide UDL implementation, we can also plan for risks that could produce greater reward or results: if we risk doing this, then we could gain that. The paragraphs that follow outline some common negative risk assessments of UDL projects, as well as the positive risks that correlate with them.

UDL isn't scientifically rigorous enough to support policy changes. In an article entitled "Belief Without Evidence? A Policy Research Note on Universal Design for Learning," Michael Murphy posits that

> no rigorous published research has demonstrated any improvement in an education intervention designed with UDL principles in mind. Furthermore, the community of

> practice around UDL appears to be hostile to questions around the rigor of analysis used to promote UDL interventions. Studies of UDL approaches do not follow best practices in terms of research design, and often solicit anecdotes rather than testing the effectiveness of the approach. (Murphy 2020)

Further, Guy Boysen examines "The troubling similarities between learning styles and universal design for learning," arguing that UDL's "proponents now claim that it can increase learning for all students in all settings" (Boysen 2021). Boysen argues that UDL is like the now-discredited theory of learning styles (that people have fixed, primary, and unchanging "best" ways in which they take in information—you have likely heard of visual, auditory, and kinesthetic learners), in that UDL seems to explain a lot in a general sense, but is inadequately supported by rigorous science.

When concerned provosts and presidents have shown me these articles, I concede that the authors' points are valid, but for reasons different than they might think. There is indeed much confusion about what UDL "looks like" in practice in higher education, not because it hasn't been studied in a methodologically-sound way, but because most applications of UDL are at the individual-instructor or -designer level, making application so idiosyncratic that comparison and pattern recognition in large data sets is problematic. Similarly, CAST itself (the organization that first codified the UDL framework and now shepherds its evolution) has engaged in maximalist rhetoric about UDL being effective "for all" learners (CAST 2024a), and has made largely unsupported claims about UDL's effectiveness as grounded in neuroscience, which rests on a simplification of the general learning process—the "three brain networks" logic described in the introduction and familiar to many adherents of UDL.

To think about the positive risk of incorporating UDL into our policies and practices, we can point to three sources of information when we plan to communicate about the rigor of the UDL framework. First, the scholarly team of Kavita Rao, Sean J. Smith, Dave Edyburn, Christine Grima-Farrell, George Van Horn, and Shira Yalon-Chamowitz who developed the *UDL Reporting Criteria* instrument (Rao et al., 2018) as well as its methodological validation (Rao et al. 2020), both of which help researchers to standardize and regularize their approaches. Second, the meta-analysis work of recent scholars who are finding repeated evidence of measurable learner benefits and gains across different types of UDL applications. The evidence from these meta-analyses suggests that large-scale UDL applications of fewer, simpler—but more consistently applied—techniques correlate with benefits in learner persistence, retention, and satisfaction (see, as examples among many, Baglieri 2020; King-Sears et al. 2023; and Zhang et al. 2023). Third, as you will discover in the next section of this chapter, adopting fewer, simpler, repeatable, measurable UDL practices to lower access barriers across all our workflows allow us to test "it's not rigorous" claims directly. In many colleges and universities, we now have compelling data about how large-scale inclusive-design efforts like UDL have reduced help-desk calls, reteaching, and process-confusion interactions in service areas like information technology, as well as in teaching spaces like classrooms, labs, and online course environments (see Jones and Sjoburg 2023).

Learners don't always choose well when given options. There is a paradox in higher education of colleagues expecting, on the one hand, that students will come into our spaces already having certain knowledge, skills, and experiences—the familiar litany of "they should have learned that in high school." On the other hand, as Paul Kirschner and Jeroen van Merriënboer argue in

"Do Learners Really Know Best?" instructors today are expected to guide or frame the self-directed learning of their students:

> [We observe] the demotion of the teacher from someone whose job it was to combine her/his knowledge within a domain combined with her/his pedagogical content knowledge so as to teach those lacking this knowledge to someone whose role is standing on the sidelines and guiding and/or coaxing a breed of self-educators. These self-educators can self-regulate and self-direct their own learning—seeking, finding, and making use of all of the information sources that are freely available to them. (Kirschner and van Merriënboer 2013)

Our learners are somehow both naïve and sophisticated. They are naïve about the ways in which learning happens effectively, in need of structure and guidance from their instructors and support staffers in our institutions. They are simultaneously sophisticated enough to understand and act on the "hidden curriculum" of strategies and practices that underlie common academic tasks like navigating which courses to take each term, seeking assistance for academic and personal issues, and reading, studying, practicing, and preparing for activities in the formal curriculum. A recent wrinkle to this conversation is the debate about the amount of scaffolding and support that is appropriate to college-level learning, with some voices calling for increased rigor (e.g., Boysen 2024) and others advocating that the variability among our learners is increasing along several lines (neurodiversity, socio-economic background, cultural relevance, and more), which argues for greater flexibility as a rule (e.g., Behling and Posey 2023).

Because the goal of UDL is to produce agentic learners—learners who are "purposeful, reflective, resourceful, authentic, strategic, and action-oriented" (CAST, 2024c)—the positive risk of applying UDL is that it allows us to start by welcoming learners from widely variable backgrounds, life circumstances, and personal attributes and eventually give them all the skills, knowledge, and tools they can use to move toward greater agency and self-direction.

Kirschner & van Merriënboer are correct: it is an urban myth that college students all just show up magically capable and experienced in how to be self-directed learners. The positive risk we can collectively take by implementing UDL at scale is to bring our learners along the path toward self-efficacy, toward what many of us call paraprofessionalism, where they eventually gain enough skills and knowledge that they can begin directing some, then almost all of their own learning inquiries. But they don't start there. I've put together a chart to show what we can gain when we take the risk to design our services, classrooms, and institutional engagements inclusively with UDL.

In figure 5.1, the horizontal axis shows learner development, from beginner through proficiency to practitioner-level skills and knowledge. The rectangular box above the horizontal axis shows an inverse relationship between designed UDL and tool use. Designed UDL is the application of UDL principles by designers, instructors, and staff members in our everyday work. It's expert-led, has tight boundaries, and choices are largely constructed by instructors or facilitators. Tool use includes affordances that allow learners to practice, such as flash cards and study guides, as well as affordances that can do work for learners, such as generative large language models (what most of us think of when we say "artificial intelligence," or AI). Early in learners' experience with new ideas or processes, their choices and options should be largely constructed for them by experts who facilitate learners' paths to basic mastery. This is "learning things the long/difficult/manual way first." As learners approach proficiency, we pare back

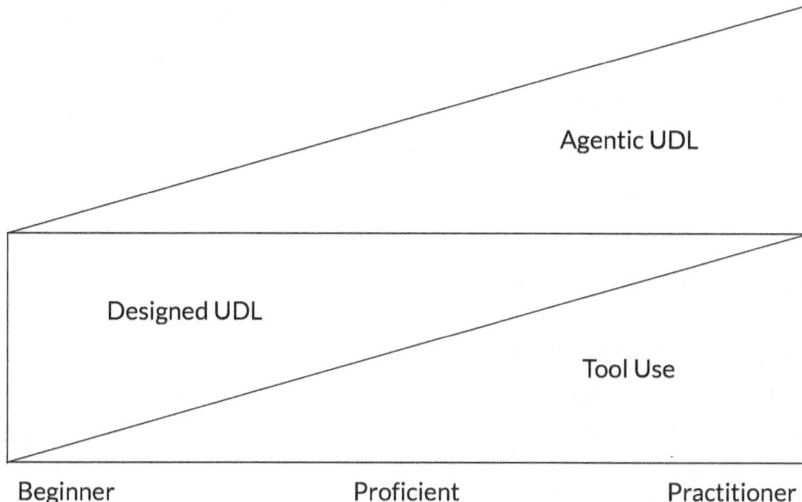

FIGURE 5.1: The "Lopsided House": Designed UDL, Agentic UDL, and Tool Use

our designed options to create space for both greater learner use of tool affordances and a concomitant rise in agentic UDL. This is represented by the sloping area above the core rectangle: turning the decision-making gradually over to the learners themselves, where learners go "above and beyond" the limitations of the learning space in increasingly self-directed ways. The "lopsided house" diagram shows agentic UDL as literally above the space of formally designed learning engagements.

In other words, when we design our spaces, places, and times in universally designed ways, we create contact points where beginners can find structure, proficient learners can begin employing tool-based shortcuts and start branching out in directions intriguing to them, and practitioner-level learners find the fewest boundaries on their actions. The "lopsided house" diagram is fractal: it can be applied at the scale of individual learning activities, sequences of activities with support staff, units within courses, courses themselves, and entire programs of study.

This process gradually shifts the risks—both negative and positive—from our institutions to the learners themselves. This aligns with our missions as colleges and universities. We want our graduates to be well-prepared professionals, ready to take on challenges in expert ways.

Planning Process Summary

The entire planning phase for a UDL-at-scale project can take months, if not years, depending on the scale of the organization and everyone's ground-level familiarity with inclusive-design principles and practices. For instance, in my work with a technical college in Wisconsin with approximately 600 staff members and instructors, the planning phase of our project to introduce UDL across all of their service touchpoints lasted for seven months, as we collaborated to create activity plans, estimate the resources available, and craft communications and risk-management plans. Before you ever set your UDL-at-scale project in motion, ensure that you have done your due diligence to initiate and plan things thoroughly and well. At this point, it will be time to act and move into Phase 3 of your project: actually doing the work.

Support Phase 3: Executing UDL at Scale Work

As you begin the implementation of your UDL-at-scale efforts, it's time to enact one of the five cultural shifts that you encountered in chapter 2. In the fourth cultural shift, our efforts move beyond the classroom and formal teaching-and-learning interactions. We start to think of the entire ecosystem of the institution and identify where learning is happening during learners' time away from our formal learning spaces and when they are working alongside support staffers like librarians, tutors, counselors, and so on. This shift helps us to establish the work of the implementation around training, championing, and establishing UDL as a component element of everyday workflows. The actual execution of your UDL scale-up project will take shape in response to your institution's culture, resources, context, and goals. Most UDL projects will share a few common elements in their execution, though, such as basic cohort training, champion training, and celebrating milestones.

3.1: Establish a UDL Cohort Training Model

A first action to take is to ensure that everyone in the organization has a clear understanding of the basics of UDL. This is the "get everyone to step two of twenty" approach that I outlined in chapter 2. Now that you have a plan in place for training everyone, assign resources to conduct the webinars, workshops, or staff-development days that give your college or university's employees a consistent high-level understanding of the UDL framework. Even if this encompasses no more than understanding the three principles of UDL (multiple means of engagement, representation, and action/expression), obtain commitment from all departments, support units, and leadership that all employees will make time to demonstrate understanding and application of core UDL knowledge. Engage your funding and support streams (e.g., time away from teaching and work practices) to measure uptake across all of your service areas: academics, support, information technology, and so on. Remember Anna Greene, Carrie Hansel, Michael Mace and their colleagues at Indiana University? When it came time to implement their project, they leveraged an existing "pinch point" with their instructional design team:

> We kind of got tired having our instructional designers crafting course materials with instructors and then having them come back from reviews by our accessibility

> colleagues with lots of comments about more work that was needed because the initial designs weren't accessible, they weren't following even the industry standards and laws that needed to apply. Multiply that times fifty-plus designers sending content to two people for review, and it quickly got out of hand. So, we decided to train everyone on digital accessibility and UDL.
>
> As we created the training materials, we realized that they [contained] information that would be useful for other teams that work with us regularly, too. This expanded into a PressBook resource, a training course that we do, and some regular sessions that we call the accessibility tip of the week. So, we share information and make sure that it's still at the top of everybody's mind.
>
> Now, a year later, people are very interested in accessibility and UDL. That was a major cultural shift. I'm seeing more people taking initiative now on accessibility in their course designs, asking different kinds of questions, and coming to me with an interest in making things accessible rather than after the fact—it's happening more in the design phase now than in the review phase. That's been a great experience, and seeing everybody on the team get really on board with it has been awesome. (Mace, personal communication November 15, 2023)

Once everyone has the basics, move on to create structures that normalize inclusive-design practices as part of the everyday work of the organization.

3.2 Find and Create UDL Champions

Over the course of three years recently, I worked with colleagues at Moraine Park Technical College (MPTC) to bring more than a hundred of their staff members, instructors, and administrators through a twelve-week UDL Champions training seminar, in which participants learned the essentials of UDL by creating, planning, and implementing their own micro-projects to apply one of the thirty-six UDL considerations to their own work for the college. Along the way, participants also learned how to talk about UDL in their shared spaces at work: department and unit meetings, shared-governance conversations, and more informal conversations with colleagues and co-workers.

In the MPTC UDL Champions series, our goals were threefold:

- Train a core group of instructors, staff, and administrators in the principles and implementation of universal design for learning (UDL);
- Provide group and individual consultations with seminar participants to identify and build out interactions in their courses and training materials according to the principles of UDL; and
- Create program-assessment and professional self-assessment instruments that can measure the direct impact of UDL-enhanced interactions on learner persistence, retention, and satisfaction. (Tobin 2024)

Seminar sessions alternated between training-focused time where participants encountered new ideas and engaged in group conversations, and individual consultations between me and each of the participants. In these consultations we talked concretely about how each person would apply UDL in their own work and reach out to their colleagues to share ideas, establish communities of interest and practice, and measure the effects of UDL adoption at various levels across the institution.

The early MPTC UDL champions were pretty lonely for a while. Imagine eight people out of a staff of more than 250 reaching out to express interest. Once we had three cohorts of completers, though, there was a critical mass of people who understood a shared vocabulary, set of practices, and goals. These champions, once established, provided a stable group of people who wanted to do the work and bring their colleagues into the work alongside them.

A second benefit of creating a group of UDL champions is to create repeatable structures for establishing competence and skills. At Atlantic Technological University (ATU) in Ireland, Maureen Haran and Niamh Plunkett established a postgraduate certificate program and a master's degree in UDL. These credentials were designed by members of their initial UDL champions cohort in collaboration with the Irish government body that oversees academic accreditation, so that their certificate and degree carry the weight of official verifications of knowledge and skill (Atlantic Technological University 2025).

3.3: Create Local Measurements and Milestones, and Celebrate Progress

UDL implementation will manifest differently across all of your organization's service points. In addition to the broad goals you have set for campus-wide UDL efforts, empower local units to track and reflect on their progress in ways that "feed up" to a larger sense of accomplishment. Provide options within and beyond campus-wide levels of implementation. This is a mindset shift that seems subtle, but which has profound effects on the adoption rate for UDL. Rather than penalizing people who don't adopt inclusive techniques, shift the narrative—and the funding—toward support. Saying "this is our collective goal; how can we support you to reach it?" is far more effective than "you must do this by December 31." Move from "must-do" to "we will support you to do." In his book on UDL for industry and the general workplace, James McKenna identifies four key practices for communications around the actual implementation work of UDL:

> **Track your actions and observations.** Document what you're doing and what the results are, including the times things don't go as planned. Don't leave it to memory; keep a record you can reference: a Google Doc, a notebook, whatever works for [your unit-level staff]. Use it as a reference tool for future designs so when you're thinking about potential barriers and countermeasures, you can refer to your notes.
>
> **Engage your learners.** Ask them how the changes you've been making have affected their experiences of learning. . . . What's working, and why? What could be improved, and do they have ideas for how? This will both inform your effort as well as communicate and reinforce your role as their partner in continuous learning.
>
> **Go and see.** Watch your learners in action. A performance improvement initiative should always translate into changes in behavior, and it's likely you or someone else close to the work is evaluating the transfer of knowledge and skills. But is that person also looking for expert-learning behaviors? Go looking for effective collaboration, peer feedback, convergent-divergent thinking, and so on. If you explicitly train an expert-learning skill in your initiative, include that in your evaluation component.
>
> **Pause and reflect.** It's great to put your head down and lean into the challenge, but it's also wise to step back, raise your gaze, and look at what you've been able to accomplish and the impact on your learners. What changes do you notice . . . in the way you and your people think and act in this work? Use this reflection to inform your expectations for yourself. (McKenna 2023, 124–125).

The actual work of making UDL-inspired changes is also the place, at the strategic level, to share and adopt the "plus one" approach from the introduction to this book. At the unit level, everyone who plans to lower access barriers with UDL will want to engage with the UDL framework at a detail level. Your UDL Champions are there to help colleagues understand how to assess learning interactions to identify gaps and barriers, and then to select and apply from the three UDL principles, nine guidelines, and their constituent thirty-six considerations. At the same time, ask everyone to identify a simpler version of the changes they are making: what's the "plus one?" If there is one way that an interaction happens now between learners and materials, other learners, instructors, support staff, and/or broader communities, how does the new UDL-inspired design help to provide just one alternative choice, path, action, or option?

UDL Champions: DeMontfort University

Recently, Kevin Merry, an internationally recognized expert on UDL, gave a webinar (Merry 2022) to share how he and his colleagues at DeMontfort University (DMU) in the United Kingdom adopted UDL across the entire institution. He shared that the situation that made his leadership team more receptive to the idea of lowering access barriers with UDL was the British government cutting support for Band 1 and Band 2 Disability Support Allowances in 2015—this is the funding that underpins the most common individual accommodations, such as note takers and individual library-support assistance. For DMU to take on these levels of individual accommodations, they calculated it would cost them roughly £5.2 million every year.

DMU could not afford to spend that much money from its own budgets, and the loss of government funding led them to ask whether there were ways to reduce the overall need for common individual accommodations. That's where Kevin and his team introduced UDL as a way to address exactly the need that had opened up. Relying on Rogers' Diffusion of Innovations theory (1962), Kevin's team recognized that DMU had already built a core group of innovators and early adopters, with the funding cut to disability accommodations providing a "tipping point" for a majority of colleagues to do the work of adopting and applying UDL principles. They found the few stakeholders whose ideas and support could really push wider adoption and gave those UDL champions platforms for sharing and building community. The UDL team also made their message "sticky," repeating it frequently so that across campus, people could remember recent conversations about UDL (and the splendid work of their UDL-champion colleagues). Third, the team enlisted the aid of their marketing department to draw up an internal-audience communication plan to provide context for the proposed changes—their student body was increasingly diverse, and the individual-accommodation model was no longer sustainable at scale without funding from the national government.

As the DMU team rolled out UDL training and support, they relied on Alyssa Davidson's four stages of communication (2013): awareness, understanding, acceptance, and commitment. This involved regular emails, a website, a resource hub, and a series of regular events with instructors and staff members—listening sessions, Q&A events, and showcases. In 2016, the annual DMU teaching and learning conference was dedicated to UDL, which showed support from leadership as well as highlighted the good work that innovators across campus were already doing.

From there, the DMU UDL implementation went through two phases. In Phase 1, three main work streams focused on quality assurance (auditing the curricula, embedding UDL into annual quality-monitoring processes), staff training and development (mandatory training, embedding UDL into learning, teaching, and assessment methodologies), and a technology tool called DMU Replay that required instructors to record and later share what happened in their live class sessions using the video-capture tool Panopto. These goals were supported by short lists of actionable "UDL quick start" ideas, such as "at least forty-eight hours in advance of teaching sessions, make learning materials available in the virtual learning environment (VLE) in a modifiable format" (Moriarty and Scarffe 2019).

Phase 2 of the DMU implementation took the form of five work streams: further development of DMU Replay/Panopto, technology to enhance UDL, teaching practices, quality enhancement, and evaluation of the project. Unsurprisingly, Kevin's team discovered that initially, the application of UDL principles was uneven across the organization, with some colleagues going only as far as recording their typical class sessions and posting them for later access. In response, Kevin created the "cheese sandwich" approach of fusing UDL principles with core pedagogical ideas to support students to achieve subject mastery and become more agentic learners. The cheese sandwich incorporates elements of the flipped-learning model to repurpose how learners spend time when they are in formal learning spaces with instructors or support staff, and how they spend time when they are working on their own. Table 5.1 shows the cheese-sandwich model that Kevin and his team created. The narrow outer columns are the "bread" indicating less time spent, and the wider middle column represents the "cheese" filling of the metaphorical sandwich where the most time is spent.

As the DMU team went through their implementation, they uncovered more reasons to continue: Left to their own devices, most staff members and instructors would "bolt on"

TABLE 5.1 The Cheese Sandwich Model of Engagement Design.
© Kevin Merry. Reproduced under CC BY license.

Pre-time	*Time with teachers and peers*	*Post-time*
Self-directed study	Teacher/peer supported study	Self-directed study
Primarily for content engagement	Primarily for supported higher-order cognitive skill development	Opportunity to revisit in-session learning
Develop lower-order cognitive skills	Explanation or demonstration of higher-order skills.	Evaluation to test capability to apply higher-order cognitive skills via formative assessment, reflecting learning outcomes
Self-assessment of lower-order cognitive skills, reflecting learning outcomes	Active practice of higher-order skills (active learning), reflecting learning outcomes	
	e-tivities reflecting learning outcomes	
	Feedback-corrected practice	
	Repeat active practice of higher-order skills	

UDL ideas to existing practices, so the UDL team worked collaboratively to embed UDL into the design of learning spaces and plans from the beginning. They also discovered patterns among learners: For instance, 50 percent of an incoming nursing-program cohort identified as dyslexic. This led to greater collaboration with disability-support and student-services colleagues throughout the implementation project.

Executing Process Summary

A last bit of summing-up advice for the executing phase of your UDL-at-scale project: communicate clear expectations from your leadership team, provide support in the form of time and resources (e.g., from your teaching center, librarians, IT team, and other support areas), phase the rollout of UDL by department or unit so that early adopters become models and champions for later ones, and start to collect narratives and key performance indicators (KPIs) in the form of aggregate data. In the next phase of your UDL project, you'll monitor its development and discover tools to help you collect information and assess your progress toward your goals.

Support Phase 4: Monitoring Your UDL Project

As you go through the phases of your UDL-at-scale implementation, it will be important to define, observe, measure, assess, and evaluate the progress and success of the various elements in which everyone in your institution is engaged. On the surface, measurement and assessment seem like challenging tasks for UDL, since it is a flexible framework where no two applications of its principles, guidelines, and considerations will happen the same way. If our UDL practitioners have voice, choice, and agency to lower access barriers in the design of their learning engagements, the biggest assessment question becomes "how can we say that X is UDL, well or poorly done, but Y is not UDL?" In other words, if UDL encompasses so many approaches that almost anything that lowers access barriers "counts," where are the boundaries? To frame an assessment strategy for a UDL-at-scale implementation, keep two ideas in mind.

First, UDL is intentional. I've heard a number of colleagues say "oh, I am already doing UDL, but I didn't yet know the name or have the details of the framework to go by." Yes, many philosophical approaches overlap with or underpin UDL (as you read about in chapter 2 with the concept of having a foundation of "mere access" to build on). However, there is no such thing as "accidental UDL." UDL efforts are made easier when practitioners are already engaged in inclusive practices; what marks efforts as UDL is the "design" part of the initialism. Design is intentional, and there's a clear and articulated reason for adopting the strategies and elements that are selected or created.

Second, UDL focuses on construct relevance. This is a term from linguistics and social science that attempts to create observations and measurements that align with and assess only (or as close to only as possible) the intended knowledge, skills, and abilities (the "construct"). Put plainly, if we wish to assess learners' math skills, we might craft a word problem about a yacht sailing at a fixed speed away from an observer atop a cliff—remember this one from high school, anyone? If the word problem contains complex vocabulary and dense logical structures, it introduces construct-irrelevant factors such as reading comprehension level, familiarity with the words in the problem, and understanding of the social or cultural referents in the problem. How many learners have seen yachts before, let alone been on one? The same approach helps us when we wish to assess the impact and effectiveness of entire implementation programs, as I'll outline below.

UDL Research in Higher Education: A Tipping Point

In 2014, Kavita Rao, Min Wook Ok, and Brian Bryant published "A Review of Research on Universal Design Educational Models," a scan of the research among various universal-design models (UDL, universal design for instruction/UDI, and universal instructional design/UID). They concluded that "the research base supporting its efficacy is in a nascent phase," and that "studies supporting the discrete checkpoints [now considerations] do not examine the application or effects of the broader framework of UDL." Most research about UDL up to 2012, when the authors collected most of their information, had to do with measurements of academic skills (using existing assessment tools to uncover impact of UDL efforts), changes in learner perceptions (how much learners felt they had greater voice, choice, agency, safety, and belonging as a result of UDL efforts), and the extent of instructor knowledge or training (how many people know about and apply UDL principles in their design and instructional practices) (Rao, Ok, and Bryant 2014).

This article, along with Dave Edyburn's 2010 "Would You Recognize UDL If You Saw It," led to the establishment of the UDL Implementation and Research Network (UDL-IRN) and eventually to the creation of the *UDL Reporting Criteria* instrument, a key stage in creating a regular, repeatable, and measurable set of data about the impact of UDL in higher education—as set out in their call for a national research agenda on UDL (Smith et al. 2019).

In your UDL-at-scale project, aim to (a) assess the effects of the work on learner *access* (see Jiménez, Graf and Rose 2007), (b) track *process-based* data about your collective knowledge and use of the UDL principles, guidelines, and considerations (see Lowrey et al. 2017; Rao and Tanners 2011), and (c) compile *outcomes-based* data about before/after comparisons of learner persistence, retention, and satisfaction. Back in 2010, Dave Edyburn's article "Would You Recognize UDL If You Saw It?" outlined a set of possible definitions and a call to research. I'd like to highlight just one of them: "we should measure the primary and secondary impact of UDL" (Edyburn 2010).

4.1: Assess UDL Impact on Access

In short, Edyburn argues that if we design learning experiences expressly to help a small population of learners—say, students with dyslexia or visual challenges—and our designs actually help only those targeted learners, then we can't call that UDL: that's assistive technology. On the other hand, if our designs have widespread secondary impact—if learners broadly benefit—then we can say they are examples of universal accessibility. Edyburn's argument gets a postscript in his 2021 update, entitled "Universal Usability and Universal Design for Learning," where he argues that

> In schools [and] classrooms that claim to implement UDL, all students would be introduced to the universal usability features of their technology devices. All students will know how to activate speech-to-text tools as well as text-to-speech tools on all common devices, even on those devices they do not personally own or use, so that they can assist others. Classroom observation should reveal that ubiquitous tools like text to speech and speech to text are used routinely by many students (i.e., secondary beneficiaries) in addition to those students whose disability requires the use of these tools (i.e., primary beneficiaries). (Edyburn 2021a)

Edyburn's call for observable outcomes aligns with the Scholarship of Teaching and Learning, or SoTL, approach to the design of learning interactions. He says that "if an intervention is used and provides benefit to the majority of students in a classroom, then perhaps there is quantifiable evidence that the intervention has universal design applications. Just to be clear, access and engagement are necessary, but not sufficient, to produce enhanced learning outcomes" (Edyburn 2021b).

4.2: Track Process-Based Data

Using SoTL concepts, we can define three ways to observe, measure, and assess the effects of UDL efforts, even ones that are radically different across various implementations.

Access to Information. All learners are introduced to multichannel access methods, such as how to use the text-to-speech functions on their mobile devices, software tools, browsers, apps, and other devices. Observation should show access tools being used routinely by many learners, not just the subset of learners for whom access tools are a necessity. This element is sometimes missing in many UDL implementations: actually showing everyone how to use the tools and options we provide. Just because we *design* the multiple means of engagement, representation, and action/expression doesn't mean learners automatically understand those structures and tools.

Expression of Depth of Knowledge (DOK). Norman Webb's DOK framework assesses whether learners can express four levels of understanding: (1) what is the knowledge? (2) how can the knowledge be used? (3) why can the knowledge be used? (4) how else can the knowledge be used? (Webb 1999). Observation of UDL-at-scale efforts should show learners seeking out information and content among various levels of complexity, and we should be able to measure greater learner agency (more learners taking action to decide the just-right level of challenge with materials and activities).

Use of Embedded Supports. UDL-informed learning interactions are more than just offering learners options; they also include just-in-time and just-in-place supports, such as the Assignment Calculator from the University of Minnesota (Peterson 2021), which helps learners to break down large assignments into smaller tasks, or context-specific help features such as pop-up definitions of terms and other interactive-media approaches. Closed captions are one form of embedded support that learners can turn on or off as they prefer. Observation should show learners seeking how-to help from both human agents (instructors, tutors, and peers) as well as broadly using the embedded supports that we design for them.

4.3: Compile Outcomes-Based Data

The last piece of the monitoring puzzle is to share what we find and adopt a standard way of talking about the observation and assessment process. In higher education and industry, we're starting to see more large-scale research studies on the effects of UDL practices, and we now have a set of *UDL Reporting Criteria*, thanks to the team of Kavita Rao, Sean J. Smith, Dave Edyburn, Christine Grima-Farrell, George Van Horn, and Shira Yalon-Chamowitz. Figure 5.2 reproduces the UDL reporting-criteria instrument; I encourage readers to download the entire instrument (Rao et al. 2018) and read the validation research surrounding it (Rao et al. 2020).

A splendid example of the monitoring, observation, and assessment process for a UDL-at-scale project is the Universal Design for Learning Today report from the Centre for Teaching & Learning Innovation team at Mohawk College in Ontario. This report showcases the college's progress from grassroots individual efforts through a scaling-up process that began with a grant-funded project to establish UDL as a design foundation for all new and revised course materials across the college. The Mohawk team's assessment work addresses three key priorities:

1. Review Mohawk College's UDL implementation to date, from both educator and learner perspectives.
2. Obtain data to inform a strategic direction for Mohawk College's UDL implementation advancement.
3. Establish recommendations and priorities for ongoing UDL implementation, with additional focus on the needs of learners from equity-deserving groups. (Centre for Teaching and Learning Innovation 2024)

FIGURE 5.2

Area and Criteria	*Y/N*	*Notes*
1. *Learner Variability and Environment*		
UDL provides guidelines for addressing learner variability and designing learning environments that are supportive for all learners. The following criteria relate to the information provided on learner and the environment in relation to the use of UDL.		
a) Participant information		
Authors describe learner variability by providing: • description of participants and general variability factors • information on specific participant characteristics (e.g., addressing literacy skills for students with a disability or a language learner, IEP objectives, disability information)		
b) Setting		
Authors describe the setting for the practice/ intervention (e.g., inclusive classroom, grade level, type of school or university).		
2. *Proactive and Intentional Design*		
An essential aspect of UDL is proactive and intentional design of curriculum, instructional, and educational environments. The following criteria relate to the use of UDL in the design phase.		
a) Addressing Barriers and/or Increasing Access		
Authors provide a description of: • specific challenges or barriers** that the practice or intervention is intended to reduce or eliminate, [and] • Issues of access being addressed by UDL. This can include barriers and/or access related to environment, curriculum, and/or instruction.		

***NOTE: Authors do not have to use the term "barrier" or "access"; other terminology that describes needs, challenges or issues being addressed can meet this criterion.*

FIGURE 5.2 (*Continued*)

Area and Criteria	*Y/N*	*Notes*
b) Designing to Address Variability		
Authors describe aspects of design that address variability. This can include a description of how flexibility, choice, or engagement will be addressed in the practice/intervention.		
c) Application of UDL Guidelines and [Considerations]		
Authors provide details about how and which of the nine UDL guidelines and/or the [thirty-six considerations] are applied to their practice/intervention. This can include information on how UDL guidelines and [considerations] are applied to goals, assessments, methods, and/or materials.		
3. Implementation and Outcomes		
Information about how the UDL-based practice is implemented and about [how] outcomes related to UDL [are] provided.		
a) Description of Implementation of Practice/Intervention		
Authors describe how the UDL-aligned practice or intervention is conducted/implemented. Authors highlight information on the UDL-based aspects of the practice and intervention (the UDL-based aspects should align with what is described in 2c).		
b) Outcomes/Findings in relation to UDL		
In addition to describing the overall outcomes of the intervention, describe UDL components in relation to outcomes for all and for specific learners (1b) (as appropriate to the purpose/RQ [research question] of the study and the inclusion of the UDL framework).		
c) Implications		
Authors describe implications of the outcomes/findings in relation to UDL-based aspects of practice/intervention.		

FIGURE 5.2: UDL Reporting Criteria, version 5.

This work was supported by a literature review, a learning management system (LMS) audit, and instructor and student surveys. The data sets in this report align specific actions taken by Mohawk College's people to the nine UDL guidelines, creating an evidentiary trace for each guideline with qualitative and quantitative data.

Monitoring Process Summary

When you are observing any UDL implementation, look for and capture the core elements described above so that you can build a research corpus of consistent and comparable descriptors for the work you and your colleagues are doing. The Big Three pieces of any UDL research or assessment should be (a) describing the participants and learning setting; (b) intentional focus on lowering access barriers through design for variability, via the UDL guidelines and considerations; and (c) results that relate directly to the UDL guidelines and considerations for specific and general participant groups. As you wrap up your UDL-at-scale project, remember to predict and plan for how to embed UDL in the everyday work of your organization.

Support Phase 5: Project Closing and Operationalization

Once you have planned, implemented, and assessed your UDL-at-scale project, it will be time to close the formal project and operationalize UDL—to make it part of your everyday workflows, processes, and policies. Getting to this point often requires years. In the Mohawk College example above, the grassroots effort that began in the early 2010s supported a grant-funded initiative in 2018 that was finally completed and assessed in 2024. How well your UDL-at-scale project "sticks" depends on three key factors as you formally close it and shift to "UDL business as usual."

Collect and analyze both qualitative and quantitative results. Throughout your scaling-up project, you and your colleagues will have created a mountain of information: trend data, narratives about processes, survey results about perceptions, and performance metrics about key indicators. Analysis of how well you met your initial project goals should support the top-line conclusion in your final reports to stakeholder groups. Not only were the goals met, but also how much did the investment of time and resources help the overall operation of the college or university?

Assign responsibility for review and assessment. In your final report, include a section on next steps beyond the formal project. List the roles on campus who will be responsible for asking their units about how they are using UDL principles in the design of new and revised learning engagements and formalize how regularly such information should be reported to the executive leadership team. We'll examine more about how to accomplish this element of post-project planning in chapter 6.

Plan your everyday UDL operations. Craft a set of workflows, guiding principles, process manuals, and the like to guide the day-to-day operations in each unit of the institution. These may already exist, thanks to your planning efforts at the beginning of the project. If not, uncover models from the grassroots, individual-effort phase before your at-scale project began (see, for example, Leichliter 2010).

A Call to Action

The phrase "universal design for learning" is broadly recognized among people in higher education (Cumming and Rose 2022). The nine guidelines, thirty-six considerations, and associated research about UDL? Not nearly as much (see Laist, et al. 2022). Most people in higher education have a passing familiarity with the idea of UDL, and less experience in actually applying the framework in an intentional and observable way. This has sometimes led to campus changes based only on faith in reported evidence from peer institutions: "the focus or emphasis seems to have shifted through educational policy, investigative efforts, and/or implementation processes. These evolutionary differences have led to an ambiguity in how the field has defined, identified, implemented, and measured UDL" (Hollingshead, Lowrey and Howery 2022). As you implement your UDL-at-scale project, adopt the stance of evidence-based planning (relying on patterns and results from peers), data-informed practice (adjusting and customizing your implementation based on information obtained from your own experiences), and operational planning (normalizing the work of inclusive design and access across all of the service units and learner touchpoints of the college or university). This process is capped by one last part of the UDL-at-scale progression, which circles all the way back to starting with the "why": making meaningful rewards that embed UDL practices into our everyday processes and work.

6

REWARD UDL

Incentive Systems

The next-to-last major shift for adopting universal design for learning (UDL) at scale is to create meaningful rewards for adopting inclusive design practices across all of your organization's service touchpoints. I'm treating this topic as a separate chapter in this book, but you should consider and implement this aspect of your scale-up efforts throughout the entire planning and implementation processes, and beyond. In this chapter, you'll start thinking in two ways simultaneously: how you can create micro-level rewards that jump-start and sustain people's initial efforts, as well as how you can operationalize rewards so that they align with your existing institutional goals and values.

The scale of reward systems correlates roughly to the number of stakeholders needed to implement the rewards. For micro-level rewards with brief duration (say, offering a faculty member a one semester course-teaching-load reduction, or assigning an inclusive project as part of a staff member's everyday work tasks for a month), existing authority, policy, and political structures are often sufficient to take action immediately. When we think about rewards for groups of employees over larger time frames and with more consistent parameters, we edge into the need to agree on changes to policy (as you saw in chapter 4) and negotiate regular, repeatable, and consistent reward processes and structures. In this chapter, you'll meet colleagues who have created both micro- and macro-level reward structures, both within and beyond the boundaries of their colleges and universities. But first, we need to examine why reward structures themselves are necessary and why "it's the right thing to do" doesn't move most people to act—even colleagues who see themselves as allies to UDL adoption.

We Do That for Which We Are Rewarded

Psychologists use a powerful metaphor to explain why humans often agree with virtuous ideas but don't act on them, sometimes for a long time. "The mind is divided in many ways, but the division that really matters is between conscious/reasoned processes and automatic/implicit processes. These two parts are like a rider on the back of an elephant. . . . Learning how to train the elephant is the secret of" getting people to act (Haidt 2006, 15). We are not always logical actors, weighing the greatest benefit to ourselves or our communities. Rather, humans only *tend* to value rewards and avoid problems. In chapter 5, I referred briefly to the mindset shift of moving leaders' messaging around UDL from "you must" compliance or requirements to "we will support you." The elephant-and-rider analogy underpins why this shift is necessary for long-term behavioral change. Avoidance of penalties in the "you must" scenario will result in compliance, but grudgingly so. Doron Dorfman, writing about disability rights, notes a paradox around how we create reward structures for desired virtuous conduct.

> Many scholars view the idea of accommodations as a redistributive scheme in the form of "positive rights." Positive rights pose affirmative duties on the state or other entities (such as private employers or places of public

> accommodations). They are thus foreign to the American legal tradition of only providing "negative rights," which prohibit interference with private behavior (such as the right to free speech or to practice one's religion). Therefore, the positive right to receive disability accommodations has been criticized by economists [as] preferable treatment given to disabled persons. (Dorfman 2020, 338–339)

Why are we talking about disability again? It's a mental mistake that our colleagues make routinely. When we say "UDL," our colleagues can think that we are talking only about accessibility, and only about the students who have formal disability-accommodation paperwork. This is one contributing factor to low engagement and action numbers in most UDL efforts. Our colleagues ask "why would we do all of this work just to help a few students? Better to wait until we get the paperwork that says what we absolutely have to do."

In other words, people form unconscious schema of "deservingness" based on whether positive rights are appropriate, consistent, and perceived to be fair. Curb cuts for wheelchair users are largely perceived as fair and necessary because wheelchair users are perceived as visibly "deserving" of the change to the built environment. Creating alternative-format content for everyone (part of baseline accessibility) is often perceived as "extra" work because there is no visible, especially deserving population for whom the benefit seems best to fit.

Finally, people tend to remember gains and losses better than savings. Add tasks to people's weekly workload, and they will perceive "more work for me." Cut funding for supplies, travel, and professional development, and people will perceive "fewer resources for me." But enact new workflows that require intentional effort but which also save overall time in addressing questions, confusion, rework, and problems (this is the argument for

UDL in a nutshell) . . . and people will *still* perceive "more work for me," even when it's not so, because the wide-scale time savings are largely invisible to individuals.

We need systemic and consistent reward systems around at-scale UDL efforts to connect the work that must be done to outcomes that are meaningful to the people doing the work. Most people agree with the goals of UDL. We should lower access barriers and create environments that welcome and support learners. Most people will also not act on those positive thoughts, staying in the mental space of "we should" and counting themselves among the virtuous because of their beliefs without having to act on the ideas, sometimes for years.

Appeals to ethical, moral, or social norms run into the tension between rationality and emotion because of people's unexamined "deservingness" biases, their general sense of fairness, and their perception of work that results in savings as still "extra" effort. All this is to say that large-scale behavioral change happens when emotional and rational rewards align. This means we must create meaningful and parallel reward structures at the individual and organizational levels.

Meaningful Individual Rewards

When asked to name rewards that are likely to motivate staff members and instructors, higher- education leaders most often cite monetary rewards (for example, stipends or salary increases) and prestige rewards (for example, recognition during all-staff events, framed certificates). While these sorts of incentives work well, the majority of meaningful rewards for UDL practice should address practitioners' everyday workflows. For example, when instructors adopt new-to-them inclusive practices and write up their experiences for sharing with colleagues, a good non-financial reward might be to bring those instructors to the front of the queue for selecting which courses to teach in the following term. Meaningful rewards, at the micro level, recognize the work that goes into adopting and applying UDL by providing temporary benefits to help make the academic lives of innovators or adopters smoother or easier. This creates both emotional and rational motivators to engage in individual UDL practices.

Reward Structures at Scale

Likewise, meaningful rewards for UDL application at scale can tap into the emotional power of peer perception and the rational power of work-related benefits. When Dara Ryder and his colleagues at AHEAD Ireland wanted to support staff members in further and higher- education institutions to adopt UDL, they worked with the Irish government to establish a UDL badge micro-credential that would be accepted by all colleges and universities toward people's job promotion schemes. Further, AHEAD and Atlantic Technological University (ATU) hosts an annual UDL National Conference for the higher- and further-education sectors in Ireland, at which educators are encouraged to share case studies and effective practices through presentations and inclusive workshops. In October of 2024, ATU's annual UDL conference included the national John Kelly Awards for UDL (sponsored by AHEAD Ireland and University College Dublin).Both the conference itself and the award for innovative practice are responses to a need for rewards at scale:

> The rapid rise of interest in UDL practice is welcome, but success brings its own challenges. The pace of new developments has led to common confusion around the use of terminology. A lack of a coherent sectoral vision for how UDL and its related frameworks fit together in harmony is evident. There appears to be a lack of strategic planning

> at institutional level on its implementation. (Ryder and Duffy 2023)

Only two years into the UDL badge program, more than a thousand practitioners hold the credential (Shevlin and Ryder 2024), and further badges in the program are on offer or in development. The key to growth and adoption has to do with scaling up the reward system. "Counting" the credential toward promotion and salary increases legitimizes the program and creates value beyond individual institutions.

In an early article outlining a successful inclusive-design effort at the University of Minnesota, David Arendale and Robert Poch outlined their approach, which encompasses elements of both micro- and macro-level rewards.

> In addition to awareness presentations, short workshops, and distribution of training materials, the following activities may be essential for sustained adoption of UDL practices: (a) travel to professional conferences related to UDL, (b) purchase of materials such as books and journals related to UDL, (c) summer stipends for those not employed at that time of year to attend workshops and work with one another on UDL, (d) overload pay for faculty and staff to work on UDL during their contract period, and (e) meaningful impact on annual evaluation and merit raise criteria. (Arendale and Poch 2008)

How to Frame and Implement UDL Rewards

As you think about how to incorporate meaningful rewards into the micro- and macro-level elements of your UDL scale-up efforts, pause to consider what our economist friends might call the "perverse incentives" of reward structures themselves. An example from an earlier type of scale-up narrative in higher education is instructive, here.

In the late 1990s and early 2000s, most of our institutions began creating online offerings. A small number of interested instructors and designers began tinkering with the then-new modality of asynchronous online learning, creating online courses here and there, organically and in a patchwork fashion. This should sound familiar: UDL is today largely at this same "early adopters" stage of uptake among most colleges and universities.

As campus leaders began to see value in offering asynchronous online programs and credentials ("It's convenient!" "We'll grow our enrollments!" "We don't have to schedule a room!"), they implemented a number of reward schemes to increase interest in developing new online courses. These rewards most often took the form of money: stipends to develop courses in the new format, buy-outs of instructor time for course development, and extra pay to teach online courses due to the perceived "extra" workload of doing so. These rewards had the intended effect: the early adopters cashed in to continue doing what they had been doing. Newer designers and instructors were attracted by the funds to develop more courses and offerings, as well (see Herman 2013).

A problem arose later, though, when online offerings became routine things. People who otherwise might have created online courses began to expect payment for their development and teaching, above and beyond the ordinary processes already in place. The incentives that initially had helped to jump-start the scaling-up efforts now, paradoxically, created a mindset that online versions of courses were somehow special, separate, and not just part of "everyday work." It took a long time for norms and cultures to shift away from this perception—today, there are still some colleges and universities who pay more for teaching online than for teaching in classrooms, but the majority of institutions today say "a course is a course, regardless of modality, and we pay the same for both."

My goal in writing this book is to make universal design for learning part of our everyday work, to help you to shift the culture in your organizations around inclusive design away from "this seems like extra effort." In this spirit, I propose a four-part rewards scheme, based on successful efforts at dozens of colleges and universities worldwide: (1) use both hard- and soft-form rewards, (2) give rewards at the institutional level for systemic changes, (3) create local rewards for truly above-and-beyond efforts, and (4) design pathways for converting rewards from hard to soft formats over time.

Use both hard- and soft-form rewards. Hard-form rewards are those in which the benefit outlasts the reward action itself. These are things like money and paying for skills training. Soft-form rewards are used up as part of the reward action. These include things like being first in line to select teaching schedules for the next term and reduced teaching loads that allow for new skill work. In order to reduce the risk that your UDL-at-scale rewards might unintentionally set UDL aside as an "extra" effort, begin your reward scheme with both hard- and soft-format rewards. Ideally, tie rewards to your UDL project goals, and frame them not as "bonuses" or "extras," but as part of the support options that are offered to everyone in order to meet the minimum criteria, as you read about in chapter 3.

Give rewards from the institutional level for systemic changes. One of the five major shifts that we've examined for scaling up UDL efforts is that we adopt fewer, broader, more strategic goals, and we measure them in terms of overall learner persistence, retention, and satisfaction. This requires a reward system that does something different from typical rewards that recognize when people go *above and beyond* their everyday responsibilities. At scale, we should reward people's efforts to incorporate UDL *into* their everyday responsibilities. Thus, rewards should apply to everyone in the organization equally. Anyone can qualify for and earn the rewards we create, and we expect that the majority of our employees will earn the rewards. Because of this, systemic rewards are often small in scope or cost but meaningful for recipients. I spoke recently with Julia Larsen and her colleagues at the University of Nebraska-Lincoln, who used this idea to splendid effect when they established UDL as an element across all of their undergraduate programs, and created incentives from their service units. "We looked to put support systems in place, for instructors who were struggling to receive support and get into the UDL habit. We're helping instructors meet the university's goals by offering UDL audits of courses and then supporting instructors as they make changes" (personal communication, August 28 2023).

Create local rewards for truly above-and-beyond efforts. UDL scaling-up efforts run the risk of watering down people's understanding of what the UDL framework actually is and does. Because at-scale efforts are necessarily focused on giving everyone in the organization a simple understanding of the UDL framework and some simple-yet-consistent actions to take, our colleagues can make the mistake of thinking that this simpler version is all that the UDL framework contains. For instance, when Kirsten Behling and I published *Reach Everyone, Teach Everyone* in 2018, I advocated for people to explain UDL not with the three principles of the framework, but to start by talking about the "plus one" approach. If there's one way an interaction happens now between learners and materials, other learners, instructors, support staff, or their communities, then make just one more way for that interaction to happen. I am pleased at how widely the "plus one" concept has been adopted by colleagues across higher education. It's become a nearly ubiquitous phrase when people talk about UDL.

I am also mildly chagrined at how widely "plus one" has been adopted because so many colleagues think that it's an end point or goal, rather than the starting point that I intended it to be.

For this reason, set aside separate funds, time, and other rewards to be administered at the local level of units and departments. While everyone in the institution is being supported to do the broad, simple things in your UDL-at-scale plan, ensure that individual designers and instructors also have support to dive more deeply into the thirty-six considerations of the UDL framework and build greater expertise and experience that goes beyond the simple expectations of your at-scale program. For example, Katrina Herold advocates for establishing UDL cohorts for advanced training, merging UDL efforts with existing teaching-quality projects, and supporting UDL ambassadors or champions at the department level (2022).

Design pathways for converting rewards from hard to soft formats over time. Consider offering both hard- and soft-form rewards early in your UDL scaling-up efforts, and advertising the hard-form rewards as limited in terms of time, number, or both. For instance, provide a choice between a monetary stipend or dedicated development time to support the work in which you want employees to engage, and note that people can receive the funds for up to three instances, after which the other "soft" rewards are still available. Limiting the number of times (or the time period during which) people can claim hard-form rewards does three good things. First, it signals that the rewards are not meant to be permanent additions to the base workload or incentive package of the organization. Second, it allows for a more rapid progression by which the desired practices become part of everyday work that is expected of everyone (as we'll examine in the next chapter). And third, it incentivizes people to act more quickly in the face of scarce rewards, speeding the adoption cycle for your UDL scale-up efforts.

A Call to Action

Examine your institution's reward structures. What are the criteria for asking part-time instructors to return to teach in future terms? For full-time staff members and instructors, for what elements of their work and professional development are they held accountable (negative risk), and for what aspects of their work are they rewarded when they increase their knowledge and skills (positive risk)?

Engage with your shared-governance structures and mid-level leadership to identify both "hard-form" rewards like funds and paid upskilling, as well as "soft-form" rewards like using work time for professional-development learning, bringing people to the front of the metaphorical line for choices like which courses to teach next term, and establishing co-learning communities across siloed institutional units. Once you have set up reward systems for UDL to happen both individually and at scale, you can take the final step that goes beyond UDL-at-scale projects: expect it throughout your organization.

7

EXPECT UDL

Next Steps Beyond Scale

Congratulations! You have a robust universal design for learning (UDL) approach in place at your institution, for which you've spent considerable amounts of time, effort, and money. The last question to answer in the UDL-at-scale process is how to lock in the gains you and your colleagues have produced. Over time, colleges and universities tend to succumb to inertia and "innovation fatigue," wherein the next new idea to come along consumes the lion's share of our attention and resources.

At the beginning of this book, I asked you to think about policies and workflows that are on the books, but which people ignore or don't even know about. Scaling up our UDL efforts is a worthy goal. Scale itself also hinders our ability to maintain the level of effort and quality that we establish in the early days of our change-management efforts. Just as no one employee can know every requirement listed in the policy manual, it's a challenge to be able to monitor and control the various and multiform ways in which our organizations implement UDL principles, as you read about in chapter 5.

In the introduction to this book, I set the goal for UDL at scale as bringing "access into our core work and identity—to make access just how we do things." In this chapter, you'll learn practical ways to set UDL into the everyday workings of your institution through the reward structures you created in chapter 6, as well as your hiring, assessment, promotion, and iterative-change processes. Along the way, you'll hear the stories of people and teams who created workflows and organizational environments that simply expect inclusive efforts as part of people's everyday work and practice.

Expectations Versus Policy

Our policy manuals are by their very nature aspirational. Policies denote desired end states, how things ought to be. Whether your institution has a slim or a prodigious set of policies, no individual employee will have an overall understanding of your entire policy *corpus*. Even those whose responsibilities include shared governance—your leadership team, faculty senate, employee union representatives, and so on—will have at best an imperfect and incomplete view and understanding of all the policies that govern the operations of your college or university.

As you've experienced in the previous chapters, UDL functions best as a framework for practice. Once it is enshrined in campus policy alongside other approaches to how we structure and implement our work, we can build out new expectations on the foundation of both the policy language we have adopted (from chapter 4) and the actions we have collectively taken to implement UDL across our service touchpoints (from chapter 5). Once there is a regular and sizeable UDL component to our collective work, the last part of the process is to put in place expectations that such efforts continue as part of our everyday practices.

In too many campus-wide efforts, reaching collective goals is framed only in terms of projects—discrete groups of tasks that have defined conclusions. We move from one big project to the next, closing each once we have "done" with particular topics or emphases. There is hope that the changes to our materials, tasks, and communities will persist, but we are already on to the next Big Idea, which seems to cycle from year to year, even term to term. Here, then, are four ways to ensure that UDL becomes part of our everyday work, truly scaling up to become a signature part of our collective identity.

1. *Expect UDL from New Hires*

It is most challenging to convince long-serving employees to change their workflows and approaches. They have been part of our institutional cultures for a long time and know that if they only delay acting for long enough, the wind will change direction and perhaps they won't have to change very much about how they do their work, if at all. Not all our more-senior staff and instructors are resistant to change, but there are enough folks with their arms folded across their chests, quietly saying "you can't make me do that," that our efforts to change institutional culture through UDL should focus on the other end of the career path.

New hires are the tip of the proverbial spear for workflow and cultural changes. As you update your new-employee onboarding, ensure UDL practices are prominently shared as expectations for the work new employees will do for your institution. In addition to saying explicitly that universally designed experiences are expected of all staff members, provide examples of how current employees have lowered access barriers through the design of their engagements with colleagues, students, and the community. For example, Maureen Haran and Niamh Plunkett at Atlantic Technological University (ATU) in Ireland have a robust campus-wide UDL program that is the result of years of work, careful advocacy, and policymaking. I spoke with them recently about how they are now able to maintain the momentum of their earlier (and smaller scope) efforts. Haran points to the establishment of a microcredential badge in UDL from AHEAD, a disability-rights advocacy organization in Ireland, as a catalyst that early adopters used as a tangible proof of core knowledge and skills:

> The other measure of progress was the number of people who have completed the UDL digital badge. We did it locally first, and then it just made sense to join in the national rollout. And not only that: a lot of our colleagues were becoming facilitators of the badge, as well. Within a two-year period, we had twenty-six colleagues across ATU become facilitators of the badge. So, we could also run local rollouts in semester two, and expect that new hires would have the UDL badge as an option for their skill set in their first years. (personal communication, January 10, 2025)

So, from a campus leader's perspective, explicitly asking new hires to adopt and demonstrate UDL knowledge and skills is a front-loading way to begin changing campus culture. Expect your new staff members and instructors to be UDL proficient. This follows from the inclusion of UDL in standard job descriptions (chapter 4) and hiring documents (chapter 5). Once you have set the expectation that all new hires will put UDL into practice, you need to hold them accountable for the expectation.

2. Expect UDL in Performance Assessment

Because UDL is not a set of summative practices that must be performed consistently in the same way every time, including expectations for UDL in the formal performance-assessment processes of the institution could be a challenging task. Fortunately, performance metrics for UDL adoption can be assessed through the lens of the categories listed in the *UDL Reporting Criteria* that we examined in chapter 5.

1. Learner Variability and Environment
    (a) Participant Information
    (b) Setting
2. Proactive and Intentional Design
    (a) Addressing Barriers and/or Increasing Access
    (b) Designing to Address Variability
    (c) Application of UDL Guidelines and Considerations
3. Implementation and Outcomes
    (a) Description of Implementation of Practice/Intervention
    (b) Outcomes/Findings in Relation to UDL
    (c) Implications (Rao et al. 2018)

Where, how often, and how consistently do employees document their work inputs, processes, and outputs according to the UDL framework? Expect that supervisors know about and can assess work performance in this way, and make reporting part of the regular observation and assessment of the work skills that employees demonstrate.

3. Expect UDL in the Promotion Process

Examine the criteria by which employees earn promotion through their career arcs, and work with your shared-governance and human resources teams to include accountability for inclusive design practices such as UDL. Changes to employment-assessment processes like faculty tenure, staff role progression, and merit/remediation structures require considerable time and deliberation, so plan to engage in these conversations as soon as there is approval from your leadership team for operationalizing UDL practices.

Also, involve employees themselves in the construction of their performance plans. As James McKenna advises, "the more [employees] understand where they are, the better they can set expectations for realistic, meaningful growth. . . . [Employees] and their leaders should co-construct performance plans to allow some autonomy in improvements and developing clear connections between individual goals and those of their team, department, and organization" (McKenna 2023, 69).

4. Embed UDL in Larger Cultural Changes

A final piece of advice for expanding beyond your UDL-at-scale project into everyday operations: embed UDL into other large cultural or institutional changes. If you are switching to a new learning management system (LMS), developing brand-new micro-credential programs, erecting a new science building on campus, or reaching out to new populations of potential students with a slick marketing campaign—in all of these scenarios and more, there is an opportunity to reinforce UDL practices. Eric Moore calls these "Trojan horse" opportunities.

> People are busy. They don't want *more* to do. Connecting to existing needs is critical: where are people on campus already concerned about things like lack of student motivation, keeping up with technology, increasing accessibility-accommodations demands, poor student retention, and the risk of lawsuits over inaccessible materials? UDL is a disruptive force. It's ultimately about bringing about culture change in higher education. This means not just changing what we do, but how we do it, and who we are.
>
> Such change begins individually, but can iteratively expand as we exert influence on those in our scope. This means being willing to challenge our social context instead of letting our social context (i.e., the status quo) absorb us. Doing so means being on the lookout for opportunities to

> help with known "pain points" and to use those as opportunities to introduce and promote UDL. (Moore 2019)

Especially after a successful UDL scaling-up project, it becomes easier to say that for new projects and systemic changes, UDL is now just another ordinary part of how you do business at your college or university. In other words, when you don't even think about bolting UDL onto existing practices, but instead it's automatically included in your planning, startup, working, assessment, and wrap-up processes—then, congratulations! You're a UDL campus.

One Step Beyond!

The institution that best exemplifies the entire process of taking UDL from grassroots to scale is one you've met a couple of times already in this book: the team at Atlantic Technological University (ATU). Led by Maureen Haran and Niamh Plunkett, their UDL journey is a splendid exemplar for other colleges and universities who want completed models to examine.

The ATU team began by examining the inequities designed into the existing Irish education model of separate special education and vocational education schools that limited educational opportunities for learners who didn't fit the normative mainstream systems of tertiary education (vocational, further, and higher education beyond secondary education). In 2017, they began building on grassroots efforts, inviting external speakers to give talks and workshops about UDL and lowering access barriers. In 2018, ATU employees began earning the UDL digital badge credential newly offered by AHEAD Ireland, the disability-advocacy organization. Throughout 2018, they observed patterns among their learners, recognizing that the majority of students at their university were working adult learners with time-poverty challenges.

By 2019, the ATU team had built recurring cohorts of UDL champions, secured funding for their pilot UDL study project, and established a formal UDL working group with the support of their campus leaders. The following year—in the teeth of the global COVID-19 pandemic—they established online UDL resources, created UDL training modules, and purchased inclusive tools like Blackboard Ally. In recent years, what had started as a pilot project grew to become an operational element of the entire university, with UDL as the focus of a celebratory conference and implemented across the institution's information technology (IT) systems and practices (Haran 2023). ATU established their UDL Centre of Excellence in 2022 and continues to expand its UDL efforts within its own units and in collaboration with partner organizations throughout Ireland, with the goal of becoming a "UDL institution." Figure 7.1 shows the timeline of UDL scale-up and adoption at ATU.

In fact, our colleagues at ATU recently went beyond the scope of this book. They recently developed and now offer a master's degree program in universal design for learning, to help ensure that new practitioners will get hired throughout the Irish tertiary education environment (Haran 2023). In 2024, AHEAD's annual conference introduced publicly for the first time the ALTITUDE National Charter for Universal Design in Tertiary Education. Along with fourteen other colleges and universities, six national agencies, the six Irish Education and Training Boards (ETBs), the Irish accreditation agencies, and AHEAD Ireland, the ATU team spearheaded the national ALTITUDE Project (2024). At the time of writing, the project has launched a nationwide conversation about scaling universal design across all functions of Ireland's tertiary sector.

Today, at ATU and throughout Irish tertiary education, UDL is an everyday element of the curriculum, design, and teaching happening everywhere—it's "just what they do." Talk about scaling up!

Atlantic Technological University: UDL Development 2017-2025

2017-2018: Information Workshops

Oct 2019: Pilot Study Project (Funding Secured from NEFTL)

2018-2019: UDL Local Rollouts & Online Resources

Dec 2019: UDL Working Group Established

Spring 2020: Module Manager

Summer 2020: UDL Module Audits

Sep 2020: Blackboard Ally Adoption

Spring 2021: SATLE Project: Conceptualizing UDL with the Student Voice

Mar 2021: Programmatic Review

May 2021: Inaugural UDL-CUA Conference: "Building a Culture of inclusion in Higher Education"

2022: Designation as a Technological University

May 2022: UDL-ATU Conference: "Conceptualizing UDL with the Student Voice"

Summer 2022: Path 4: National Lead on 3 Projects

Oct 2022: New Programme: Post-Graduate Certificate & Master's in UDL

Nov 2022: Winner of John Kelley Award for Collaboration in UDL (2022-2024)

May 2023: Peer Networks Established across ATU

May 2023: National Workshop Series:
Digital Inclusion
Inclusive Curriculum Design
Inclusive Module Reviews

May 2023: Student Empowerment Project

June 2023: ATU/MTU Collaborative Conference: "Overcoming Obstacles to Enhance & Sustain UDL Collaboration in Tertiary Education"

Sep 2023: West/Northwest UD Regional Hub Established with Donegal ETB, MSLETB, & GRETB

Mar 2024: UDL Student Digital Badge Student Empowerment Project

Mar 2024: Launch of ALTIT**UD**E Charter

Oct 2024: ATU-UDL Conference: "Practical Approaches to Embedding UDL in Tertiary Education"

Spring 2025: International EQUIP Collaborative, Humber Polytechnic, Toronto, Canada

FIGURE 7.1: ATU UDL Development 2017–2024. Reproduced with permission.

A Call to Action

Don't take my word that UDL just works. I am clear-eyed about what UDL can—and can't—do for our colleges and universities. I am what the parliamentarians would call "the loyal opposition" on many of the elements within the UDL framework. The lesson here is to test the claims and processes from this book yourself, and then . . .

Roll up your sleeves. Recent critiques of the UDL framework deserve our attention and careful responses. Ling Zhang and a team of psychologists recently examined the uneven nature of UDL implementations, finding that most at-scale projects have focused on multiple means of representation (the portion of UDL closest to existing accessibility mandates) and less so on designing multiple means of engagement, or of action & expression (Zhang et al. 2024). In order to strengthen the research base, especially for less-frequently-applied UDL considerations, our "systematic UDL implementation[s] guided by established theories" (Zhang et al. 2024) are important building blocks for the field of UDL studies. And the whole-campus reports are starting to come out now.

Sara Humphreys at the University of Sydney in Australia recently presented scaling-up strategies from her institution's UDL-at-scale project, noting lessons for scaling up and expanding beyond an initial UDL project that chime well with the progression I've pulled together in this book:

> Avoid the UDL [initialism]: use "universal design for learning" where possible. The entire UDL framework (thirty-six considerations) can be overwhelming, so ask questions instead. Cultivate a shift in thinking and develop a shared language around change. Start with small changes (the "plus-one" approach). Be transparent with your colleagues

> and students about the intent behind design changes. Know what you want change to look like: gather data. Start where you know you will have most success. Celebrate your UDL champions: share their stories. (Humphreys 2023)

In this book, it has been my pleasure to celebrate the UDL champions across the world who have actually done it. Their UDL-at-scale projects are testaments to what is possible when everyone works together toward common goals. But nothing will change without a clear need for things to be different. So, scale up, then scale out. When you accomplish any of the stages of your UDL-at-scale project, you and your team are now mentors for others. Share your data, approaches, and results in white papers, articles, e-books, workshops, seminars, and conferences.

Conclusion

As part of the research for this book, I talked with a colleague who runs the disability-support team at a specialized postsecondary organization that trains professionals in the justice, public safety, and social services fields—medics, fire crews, law-enforcement officers, and the like. Our colleague, who requested anonymity, had attended a UDL Institute Day offered by a nearby university at which I had been invited to speak.

They told me that they had been successful in obtaining their senior leadership's buy-in for adopting UDL across their curriculum, design, and service areas, largely because "we're starting to move away from the individual-accommodations model," which is straining under increased demand from learners. They shared that at their institution the administration began getting pushback from instructors who were feeling "inundated when 30 percent to 50 percent of the students in each class have individual accommodations—and it still doesn't catch everyone who would benefit from lowered barriers." In past years, instructors were used to making individual accommodations for one or two learners in each class. Now that the number is climbing toward half of all learners, the individual-accommodation model is becoming unsustainable. This realization unlocked executive support for finding patterns, assuming learner variability, and applying UDL across the organization's course designs, services, marketing, and outreach efforts. They convened a UDL team, eventually crafting a *Comprehensive Guide to Applying Universal Design for Learning* to guide their colleagues and their institution.

In the introduction to this book, I talked about the "good news" of more learners—and more varied kinds of learners—seeking higher education than ever before. This is a splendid point on which to end this book. We don't typically engage in systemic cultural and technical changes only because they are the right things to do or because they align with our mission and values. Rather, we tend to act systemically when conditions change around us, when we can see clear challenges or predict tougher times ahead.

In many colleges and universities all around the world right now, conditions are changing around us. We are welcoming more learners and plan to welcome even more. After the "demographic cliff" of declining enrollments between 2010 and 2025, beginning in 2028, we will see the largest worldwide crop of 18-year-old traditional college freshmen ever, and numbers are predicted to rise all through the 2030s (National Center for Educational Statistics 2025).

So, whether you are looking to minimize the negative risk of lawsuits and bad publicity surrounding accessibility complaints, or you wish to address declining enrollments by helping to keep the students you've already admitted at higher rates, or you are responding to changing patterns among your learners—a UDL-at-scale project addresses some of our most pressing challenges in higher education by making access part of our everyday work. It doesn't need to be perfect, either. UDL at scale is a complex undertaking. It is both a technical and a cultural change. And it's worth the effort: UDL at scale pays us back in increased learner persistence, retention, and satisfaction. UDL is good business.

WORKS CITED

Ableser, J., and Moore, C. 2018, September 10. "Universal Design for Learning and Digital Accessibility: Compatible Partners or a Conflicted Marriage?" *EDUCAUSE Review.* https://er.educause.edu/articles/2018/9/universal-design-for-learning-and-digital-accessibility-compatible-partners-or-a-conflicted-marriage.

Adams, B. 2023. CITL Launching New UDL Team. *Center for Innovation in Teaching & Learning News.* University of Illinois. https://web.archive.org/web/20250418101212/https://citl.illinois.edu/about-citl/news/2023/05/04/citl-launching-new-udl-team.

Al-Azawei, A., Parslow, P., and Lundqvist, K. 2017. "The Effect of Universal Design for Learning (UDL) Application on E-learning Acceptance: A Structural Equation Model." *International Review of Research in Open and Distributed Learning* (IRRODL), *18*(6): 54–87. https://files.eric.ed.gov/fulltext/EJ1155806.pdf.

ALTITUDE Project. 2024. *ALTITUDE: The National Charter for Universal Design in Tertiary Education.* Dublin, IE: AHEAD Educational Press. https://www.atu.ie/app/uploads/2024/12/altitude-charter-supplied-digital.pdf.

Arendale, D., and Poch, R. 2008. "Using Universal Design for Administrative Leadership, Planning, and Evaluation." In *Pedagogy and Student Services for Institutional Transformation: Implementing Universal Design in Higher Education,* edited by J. L Higbee and J. Goff. University of Minnesota. 419–436. https://files.eric.ed.gov/fulltext/ED503835.pdf.

Atlantic Technological University (ATU). 2025. "Universal Design for Learning Post-Graduate Certificate Programme." Atlantic Technological University. https://www.atu.ie/courses/postgraduate-certificate-universal-design-for-learning.

Baglieri, S. 2020. "Toward Inclusive Education? Focusing a Critical Lens on Universal Design for Learning." *Canadian Journal of Disability Studies*, 9(5): 42-74. https://cjds.uwaterloo.ca/index.php/cjds/article/view/690.

Beach, A., Sorcinelli, M. D., Austin, A., and Rivard, J. 2016. *Educational Development in the Age of Evidence*. Stylus Publishing.

Bedi, P., Bowen, S., Fritz, J., and Lightfoot, C. 2023. "2024 EDUCAUSE Top 10 #6: Meeting Students Where They Are: Providing Universal Access to Institutional Services." *EDUCAUSE Review*, October 23. https://er.educause.edu/articles/2023/10/2024-educause-top-10-6-meeting-students-where-they-are.

Behling, K., and Linder, K. 2017. "Collaborations Between Centers for Teaching and Learning and Offices of Disability Services: Current Partnerships and Perceived Challenges." *Journal of Postsecondary Education and Disability*, 30(1): 5–15.

Behling, K., and Posey, A. 2023. "UDL in American Colleges and Universities: A Common Pathway to Success." In *Handbook of Higher Education and Disability*. https://www.elgaronline.com/edcollchap/book/9781802204056/book-part-9781802204056-42.xml.

Berhtram, C., Gutirerez, P., and Sadler, A. 2024. "Equity and Inclusion Project Management Checklist." *Digital Education News*. Stanford University. https://digitaleducation.stanford.edu/news/equity-and-inclusion-project-management-checklist.

Blasey, J., Wang, C., and Blasey, R. 2023. "Accommodation Use and Academic Outcomes for College Students with Disabilities." *Psychological Reports*, *126*(4): 1891–1909. https://doi.org/10.1177/00332941221078011.

Bogdan, G. 2018. *Universal Design for Learning*. Greensboro College. https://www.greensboro.edu/academics/student-success/universal-design-for-learning/.

Borghans, L., and Golsteyn, B. H. H. 2015. "Susceptibility to Default Training Options Across the Population." Institute for the Study of Labor (IZA) Discussion Paper 9180. http://ftp.iza.org/dp9180.pdf.

Boston College. 2025. *Universal Design for Learning*. https://cteresources.bc.edu/documentation/universal-design-for-learning/.

Bowen, J. 2003. *A History of Western Education*. Routledge.

Bowery, R., and Houston, L. 2017. "Reaching All Learners by Leveraging Universal Design for Learning in Online Courses." *EDUCAUSE Review*, December 17. https://er.educause.edu/articles/2017/12/reaching-all-learners-by-leveraging-universal-design-for-learning-in-online-courses.

Boysen, G. A. 2021. "Lessons (Not) Learned: The Troubling Similarities Between Learning Styles and Universal Design for Learning." *Scholarship of Teaching and Learning in Psychology*. *10*(2): 207-221. https://doi.org/10.1037/stl0000280.

Boysen, G. A. 2024. "A Critical Analysis of the Research Evidence Behind CAST's Universal Design for Learning Guidelines." *Policy Futures in Education, 22*(7): 1219-1238 https://journals.sagepub.com/doi/10.1177/14782103241255428.

Breckenridge, J.P., Gray, N., Toma, M., Ashmore, S., Glassborow, R., Stark, C., and Renfrew, M. J. 2019. "Motivating Change: A Grounded Theory of How to Achieve Large-scale, Sustained Change, Co-created with Improvement Organisations Across the UK." *BMJ Open Quality, 8*(2). https://bmjopenquality.bmj.com/content/8/2/e000553.abstract.

Brown, W. 2018. "The Chief Information Officer in Higher Education, 2018 Report." *EDUCAUSE Center for Analysis and Research (ECAR) Research Reports*. https://library.educause.edu/resources/2018/12/the-chief-information-officer-in-higher-education-2018-report.

Burgstahler, S., and Vinten-Johansen, C. 2017. "Seven Steps Toward IT Accessibility Compliance." *EDUCAUSE Review*, September 17. https://er.educause.edu/articles/2017/9/seven-steps-toward-it-accessibility-compliance.

California State University. 2013. "Accessible Technology Initiative Policy. Policy 16173563." *CSU System Policy Manual*. https://calstate.policystat.com/policy/16173563/latest.

California State University. 2024. *Accessible Technology Initiative (ATI)*. https://ati.calstate.edu/.

[Cameron, J.] 2016. Basic 4 of Accessibility. Academic Web Accessibility. Kennesaw State University. https://campus.kennesaw.edu/faculty-staff/academic-affairs/curriculum-instruction-assessment/digital-learning-innovations/academic-web-accessibility/basic-accessibility-solutions/basic-four-accessibility.php.

Capp, M. J. 2017. "The Effectiveness of Universal Design for Learning: A Meta-analysis of Literature Between 2013 and 2016." *International Journal of Inclusive Education, 21*(8). 791–807. https://doi.org/10.1080/13603116.2017.1325074.

CAST 2008. *Universal design for learning guidelines version 1.0 [graphic organizer]*. CAST. https://udlguidelines.cast.org/binaries/content/assets/udlguidelines/udlg-v1-0/udlg_graphicorganizer_v1-0.pdf.

CAST 2024a. *The UDL Guidelines.* Version 3.0. Update 31 Jul. 2024. https://udlguidelines.cast.org/.

CAST. 2024b. "Consideration 5.2: Use Multiple Tools for Construction and Composition." *Universal Design for Learning Guidelines* version 2.2. https://udlguidelines.cast.org/action-expression/expression-communication/construction-composition.

CAST. 2024c. *The Goal of UDL: Learner Agency.* https://udlguidelines.cast.org/more/udl-goal/.

Centre for Teaching & Learning Innovation. 2024. *Universal Design for Learning Today: Measuring Mohawk College's Implementation: Research Project Report.* Mohawk College. https://www.mohawkcollege.ca/sites/default/files/CTL/documents/UDL%20Today-Research%20Report-FINAL.pdf.

Clear, J. 2018. *Atomic Habits: An Easy & Proven Way to Build Good Habits & Break Bad Ones.* Avery.

Council for Exceptional Children. 2011. *New Guidelines for Universal Design for Learning Provide a Roadmap for Educators and Educational Publishers.* https://web.archive.org/web/20120116035812/http://www.cec.sped.org/AM/Template.cfm?Section=Home&CAT=none&CONTENTID=10573&TEMPLATE=/CM/ContentDisplay.cfm.

Cullen, S. 2018. "Accessibility: A Shared Campus Responsibility Best Accomplished with Executive Support." *EDUCAUSE Review*, January 18. https://er.educause.edu/articles/2018/1/accessibility-a-shared-campus-responsibility-best-accomplished-with-executive-support.

Cumming, T. M., and Rose, M. C. 2022. "Exploring Universal Design for Learning as an Accessibility Tool in Higher Education: A Review of the Current Literature." *Australian Educational Researcher*, 49: 1025–1043. https://doi.org/10.1007/s13384-021-00471-7.

Davidson, A. 2013. *Communicate Your Change: a 4-Factor Model for Change Management Communication.* PhD diss., University of Minnesota: https://conservancy.umn.edu/server/api/core/bitstreams/75b502ee-18e3-4fb2-baa0-9b3b23d302ed/content.

Davies, P. L., Schelly, C. L., and Spooner, C. L. 2013. "Measuring the Effectiveness of Universal Design for Learning Intervention in Postsecondary Education." *Journal of Postsecondary Education and Disability*, *26*(3): 195–220. https://files.eric.ed.gov/fulltext/EJ1026883.pdf.

DeSilva, E., Nemeroff, A., and Lopez, P. 2017. "Igniting a Universal Design Mindset on Campus." *EDUCAUSE Review*, December 17.

https://er.educause.edu/articles/2017/12/igniting-a-universal-design-mindset-on-campus.

Dorfman, D. 2020. "[Un]Usual Suspects: Deservingness, Scarcity, and Disability Rights." *UC Irvine Law Review, 10*(2): 557–618. https://escholarship.org/content/qt5qc9150h/qt5qc9150h.pdf.

EDUCAUSE. 2023. *2024 EDUCAUSE Top 10 IT Issues, Technologies, and Trends.* https://www.educause.edu/research-and-publications/research/top-10-it-issues-technologies-and-trends.

Edyburn, D. L. 2010. "Would You Recognize Universal Design for Learning If You Saw It? Ten Propositions for New Directions for the Second Decade of UDL." *Learning Disabilities Quarterly, 33*(1): 33–41.

Edyburn, D. L. 2021a. "Ten Years Later: Would You Recognize Universal Design for Learning If You Saw It?" *Intervention in School and Clinic, 56*(5): 308–309. https://doi.org/10.1177/1053451220963114.

Edyburn, D. L. 2021b. "Universal Usability and Universal Design for Learning." *Intervention in School and Clinic, 56*(5): 310–315. https://doi.org/10.1177/1053451220963082.

Fitchburgh State University. 2022. *2021–2022 Unit Annual Report Division of Academic Affairs Unit: Business.* https://www.fitchburgstate.edu/sites/default/files/documents/2022-07/Administrative%20Annual%20Report%20Business%20AY2122.pdf.

Fovet, F. 2021. "UDL in Higher Education: A Global Overview of the Landscape and its Challenges." In *Handbook of Research on Applying Universal Design for Learning Across Disciplines: Concepts, Case Studies, and Practical Implementation.* IGI Global.

Fovet, F. 2022. "UDL Masterclass: What now? Synthesising Strategic Tips for the Next Decade of UDL Development." Australian Disability Clearinghouse on Education and Training (ADCET). https://www.adcet.edu.au/resource/11222/udl-masterclass.

Goodwin University. 2015. *About Goodwin: Our Mission.* https://www.goodwin.edu/about/mission.

Government of Ontario. 2005. *Accessibility for Ontarians with Disabilities Act* (AODA). https://www.aoda.ca/the-act/.

Greensboro College. 2022. *Strategic Plan 2022–2027.* https://www.greensboro.edu/about/strategic-plan/.

Haidt, J. 2006. *The Happiness Hypothesis: Finding Modern Truth in Ancient Wisdom.* Basic Books. https://www.happinesshypothesis.com/.

Haran, M. 2023. "The Pendulum Swing in Inclusive Tertiary Education: Identifying the Centrifugal Forces and Factors." *The AHEAD Journal,*

1(16). https://www.ahead.ie/journal/The-Pendulum-Swing-in-Inclusive-Tertiary-Education--Identifying-the-Centrifugal-Forces-and-Factors.

Herman, J. 2013. "Faculty Incentives for Online Course Design, Delivery, and Professional Development." *Innovative Higher Education, 38*(1): 397–410. https://link.springer.com/article/10.1007/s10755-012-9248-6.

Herold, K. M. 2022. "Best Practices for Institution Wide Implementation of Universal Design for Learning in Higher Education." PhD diss., Northeastern University. https://repository.library.northeastern.edu/files/neu:4f17qh056.

Hollingshead, A., Lowrey, K. A., and Howery, K. 2022. "Universal Design for Learning: When Policy Changes Before Evidence." *Educational Policy*, 36(5), 1135–1161. https://doi.org/10.1177/0895904820951120.

Humphreys, S. 2023. *Implementing Universal Design for Learning (UDL) at the University of Sydney: Lessons Learned and Scaling Strategies.* Australian Disability Clearinghouse on Education and Training (ADCET). https://www.adcet.edu.au/resource/11434/adcet-webinar-implementing-universal-design-for-learning-udl-at-the-university-of-sydney-lessons-learned-and-scaling-strategies.

Jiménez, T. C., Graf, V. L., and Rose, E. 2007. "Gaining Access to General Education: The Promise of Universal Design for Learning." *Issues in Teacher Education, 16*(2): 41–54. https://eric.ed.gov/?id=EJ796250.

Jones, A., and Sjoberg, A. 2023. "Weaving the Thread of UDL Throughout the Curriculum Tapestry." Webinar presentation. *UDL Symposium.* Australian Disability Clearinghouse on Education and Training (ADCET). https://www.adcet.edu.au/resource/11490/udl-symposium-4c-weaving-the-thread-of-udl-throughout-the-curriculum-tapestry.

Kearney, D. B. 2022. *Universal Design for Learning (UDL) for Inclusion, Diversity, Equity, and Accessibility (IDEA).* eCampus Ontario. https://ecampusontario.pressbooks.pub/universaldesign/.

King-Sears, M. E., Stefanidis, A., Evmenova, A. S., Rao, K., Mergen, R. L., Owen, L. S., and Strimel, M. M. 2023. "Achievement of Learners Receiving UDL Instruction: A Meta-analysis." *Teaching and Teacher Education, 122*(1). https://doi.org/10.1016/j.tate.2022.103956.

Kirschner, P. A., and van Merriënboer, J. J. G. 2013. "Do Learners Really Know Best? Urban Legends in Education." *Educational Psychologist, 48*(3), 169–183. https://doi.org/10.1080/00461520.2013.804395.

Laist, R., Sheehan, D., and Brewer, N., eds. 2022. *UDL University: Designing for Variability across the Postsecondary Curriculum.* CAST Publishing.

Langostine, T. 1963. *The Vinegar Works: Three Volumes of Moral Instruction.* Simon & Schuster.

Leichliter, M. E. 2010. "A Case Study of Universal Design for Learning Applied in the College Classroom." PhD diss., West Virginia University. https://researchrepository.wvu.edu/etd/4625.

Lowrey, K. A., Hollingshead, A., Howery, K., and Bishop, J. B. 2017. "More Than One Way: Stories of UDL and Inclusive Classrooms." *Research and Practice for Persons with Severe Disabilities*, 42(4): 225–242. https://journals.sagepub.com/doi/10.1177/1540796917711668.

Mace, R. L., Hardie, G. J., and Place, J. P. 1989. *Accessible Environments: Toward Universal Design.* Center for Accessible Housing, North Carolina State University.

MacGuire, M. J. 2023. "The Vision Matures: Completing the Campus and Creating a Research Institute." *Landmark College Archives: College History.* https://www.landmark.edu/library/landmark-college-archives/college-history/the-vision-matures-completing-the-campus-and-creating-a-research-institute.

Manly, C. A. 2022. "Utilization and Effect of Multiple Content Modalities in Online Higher Education: Shifting Trajectories toward Success through Universal Design for Learning." PhD diss., University of Massachusetts Amherst. https://scholarworks.umass.edu/dissertations_2/2408.

McKenna, J. 2023. *Upskill, Re-Skill, Thrive: Optimizing Learning and Development in the Workplace.* CAST Publishing.

Meo, G., and Currie-Rubin, R. 2015. "CAST's UDL Implementation Phases." CAST Publishing. https://web.archive.org/web/20240926193112/https://www.cast.org/binaries/content/assets/cast/downloads/overview_implementation.pdf.

Merry, K. 2022. "Institution-wide Approaches to Embedding UDL." Posted February 24, 2022, by University College Cork. YouTube, 1:00:50.. https://youtu.be/Ce03AbEY9GM.

Moore, E. J. 2019. *From Silos to Systems: Navigating the Growth of UDL in Higher Ed. Conference presentation.* CAST UDL Symposium. https://drive.google.com/drive/folders/1qwArgX-ItxMIs5BQvnwYAYoOwVPqdTzh.

Moriarty, A. 2018. "Developing an Institutional Approach to UDL—Big Bang or Slow Burn?" *AHEAD Journal* 1.8. https://www.ahead.ie/journal/Developing-an-Institutional-Approach-to-UDL-Big-Bang-or-Slow-Burn.

Moriarty, A., and Scarffe, P. 2019. "Universal Design for Learning and Strategic Leadership: A Whole-university Approach to Inclusive

Practice." In *Transforming Higher Education through Universal Design for Learning*, edited by S. Bracken and K. Novak Routledge.

Moriarty, S. 2018. "Building a Culture of Accessibility in Higher Education." *EDUCAUSE Review*, July 18. https://er.educause.edu/blogs/2018/7/building-a-culture-of-accessibility-in-higher-education.

Murphy, M. P. 2020. "Belief Without Evidence? A Policy Research Note on Universal Design for Learning." *Policy Futures in Education*, *19*(1): 7–12. https://doi.org/10.1177/1478210320940206.

[NCAEM] National Center on Accessible Educational Materials 2020. *Higher Education Critical Components of the Quality Indicators for the Provision of Accessible Educational Materials Accessible Technologies*. National Center on Accessible Educational Materials. https://aem.cast.org/get-started/resources/2020/higher-education-critical-components-of-the-quality-indicators-for-the-provision-of-accessible-educational-materials--accessible-technologies.

[NCES] National Center for Education Statistics. 2025. "Projections of Education Statistics to 2030." https://nces.ed.gov/programs/PES/section-5.asp

Nave, L. host 2018. *Think UDL*. Episode 1. "Why learn? with Eric Moore." Podbean, December 18. Podcast, 39 min., 28 sec. https://thinkudl.org/episodes/episode-1-why-learn-eric-moore.

Nave, L. host 2019. *Think UDL*. Episode 24. "Whole campus UDL buy-in with Bryan Berrett." Podbean, November 19. Podcast, 22 min., 31 sec. https://thinkudl.org/episodes/whole-campus-udl-buy-in-with-bryan-berrett.

Nelson, L. L., and Basham, J. D. 2014. "A Blueprint for UDL: Considering the Design of Implementation." Universal Design for Learning Implementation and Research Network (UDL-IRN). https://www.dropbox.com/scl/fi/e742muno32p8oodxe6bgs/A_Blueprint_for_UDL_Considering_the_Desi.pdf?rlkey=77r7yva2de57uwey7npw4dxkc&dl=0.

New Hampshire Department of Education. 2019. *New Hampshire UDL Innovation Network: Year 2 (2019) Report*. CAST Publishing. https://www.education.nh.gov/sites/g/files/ehbemt326/files/inline-documents/udl-year2report.pdf.

Novak, K., and Rodriguez, K. 2018. *UDL Progression Rubric*. CAST Publishing. https://www.novakeducation.com/hubfs/Resources/UDL_Progression_Rubric.pdf.

Olaussen, E. J., Heelan, A., and Knarlag, K. A. 2019. "Universal Design for Learning—License to Learn: A Process for Mapping a Universal Design for Learning Process onto Campus Learning." In *Transforming Higher Education through Universal Design for Learning*, edited by S. Bracken and K. Novak. Routledge. 11–32.

Olsen, A. 2023. "Adapting Communication for Every Student Using Universal Design for Learning." In *D'Youville University: Lowering Barriers across Campus with UDL and UDL Champions Showcase.* Posted November 9, 2023, by Thomas Tobin. YouTube. https://www.youtube.com/watch?v=PHr4YjXwjoE&t=5287s.

Peterson, K. 2021. *Assignment Calculator.* University of Minnesota Libraries. https://www.lib.umn.edu/services/ac.

Pittman, C., and Tobin, T. 2022. "Academe has a lot to learn about how inclusive teaching affects instructors." *Chronicle of Higher Education*, February 22. https://www.chronicle.com/article/academe-has-a-lot-to-learn-about-how-inclusive-teaching-affects-instructors.

Project Management Institute (PMI). 2021. *A Guide to the Project Management Body of Knowledge (PMBOK Guide)*. Seventh Edition. PMI Publishing.

Quality and Qualifications Ireland (QQI). 2018. *Quality Assuring Assessment Guidelines for Providers.* Version 2. https://www.qqi.ie/sites/default/files/2021-10/quality-assuring-assessment-guidelines-for-providers-revised-2013.pdf.

Quirke, M., McGuckin, C., and McCarthy, P. 2024. *Adopting a UDL Attitude within Academia: Understanding and Practicing Inclusion across Higher Education.* Routledge.

Rao, K. 2021. "Inclusive Instructional Design: Applying UDL to Online Learning." *Journal of Applied Instructional Design*, 10(1). https://edtechbooks.org/jaid_10_1/preparing_teachers_f.

Rao, K., Ok, M. W., and Bryant, B. R. 2014. "A Review of Research on Universal Design Educational Models." *Remedial and Special Education*, 35(3): 153–166. https://doi.org/10.1177/0741932513518980.

Rao, K., Ok, M. W., Smith, S. J., Evmenova, A. S., and Edyburn, D. 2020. "Validation of the UDL Reporting Criteria with Extant UDL Research." *Remedial and Special Education*, 41(4): 219–230. https://journals.sagepub.com/doi/10.1177/0741932519847755.

Rao, K., Smith, S. J., Edyburn, D., Grima-Farrell, C., Van Horn, G., and Yalon-Chamovitz, S. 2018. *UDL Reporting Criteria.* Report developed by a working group of the Universal Design for Learning Implementation and Research (UDL-IRN) Research Committee. https://web.archive.org/web/20240623022336/https://udl-irn.org/udl-reporting-criteria/.

Rao, K. and Tanners, A. 2011. "Curb Cuts in Cyberspace: Universal Instructional Design for Online Courses." Journal of Postsecondary Education and Disability, 24(3): 211–229. https://eric.ed.gov/?id=EJ966125.

Rogers, E. M. 1962. *Diffusion of Innovations*. Macmillan Publishing.

Rose, D., and Meyer, A. 2002. *Teaching Every Student in the Digital Age*. Association for Supervision and Curriculum Development. https://archive.org/details/teachingeverystu0000rose.

Rose, D., Ralabate, P., and Meo, G. 2010. *The Five Phases of the UDL Implementation Process: Tools to Guide Your Journey*. CAST. https://www.livebinders.com/media/get/MjA4MzM2NjI=.

Ryder, D., and Duffy, L. 2023. "Universal Design: All Things to All People? Creating Collective Agency through Stakeholder Dialogue." *AHEAD Journal*, 1(16). https://www.ahead.ie/journal/Universal-Design-All-Things-to-All-People-Creating-Collective-Agency-through-Stakeholder-Dialogue.

Schottmiller, C. 2024. "Accessible Instructional Materials for Student Equity: Large-Scale Collaborations." Conference presentation. *Making Change, Taking Space* virtual gathering. https://drive.google.com/drive/folders/16KWHoMMMfZ3Cy2IKFrAONxyGvjUZjpK9.

Service, O., Hallsworth, M., Halpern, D., Algate, F., Gallagher, R., Nguyen, S., Ruda, S., and Sanders, M. 2014. *EAST: Four Simple Ways to Apply Behavioural Insights*. Behavioural Insights, Ltd. https://www.bi.team/wp-content/uploads/2015/07/BIT-Publication-EAST_FA_WEB.pdf.

Shachmut, K. 2021. "Asking the right questions for procuring inclusive, accessible technology." *EDUCAUSE Review*, October 21. https://er.educause.edu/articles/2021/10/asking-the-right-questions-for-procuring-inclusive-accessible-technology.

Shevlin, M., and Ryder, D. 2024. *AHEAD Annual Report 2023*. AHEAD. https://www.ahead.ie/userfiles/files/shop/free/AHEAD_Report_2023%20supplied%20-%20digital.pdf.

Smith, L. W. 2000. "Stakeholder Analysis: A Pivotal Practice of Successful Projects." Paper presented at Project Management Institute Annual Seminars & Symposium, Houston, TX. Project Management Institute. https://www.pmi.org/learning/library/stakeholder-analysis-pivotal-practice-projects-8905.

Smith, S. J., Rao, K., Lowrey, K. A., Gardner, J. E., Moore, E., Coy, K., Marion, M., and Wojcik, B. 2019. "Recommendations for a National Research Agenda in UDL: Outcomes from the UDL-IRN Preconference on Research." *Journal of Disability Policy Studies, 30*(3): 174–185. https://psycnet.apa.org/record/2019-64165-006.

Student Wellness & Accessibility Centre. 2020. *From Accessibility to Universal Design for Learning.* Humber Polytechnic. https://humber.ca/student-life/swac/accessible-learning/information-faculty/additional-resources/accommodation-to-UDL.

Sull, D., and Sull, C. 2018. "With Goals, FAST Beats SMART." *MIT Sloan Management Review*, June 18. https://sloanreview.mit.edu/article/with-goals-fast-beats-smart/.

Tagg, J. 2019. *The Instruction Myth: Why Higher Education is Hard to Change, and How to Change It.* Rutgers University Press. https://www.rutgersuniversitypress.org/the-instruction-myth/9781978804456/.

Takahaski, R. (1996). "Reed: A Middle Course." *Maverick Colleges Fourteen Notable Experiments in American Undergraduate Education.* 2nd ed. Utah Education Policy Center. 18-21. https://ocw.mit.edu/courses/es-291-learning-seminar-experiments-in-education-spring-2003/12f407263a1ca264d8ba263fadd2baab_MITES_291S03_reed_mid.pdf.

Thibodeau, T. 2021. "The Science and Research Behind the UDL Framework." *Novak Education*, September 25. https://www.novakeducation.com/blog/the-science-and-research-behind-the-udl-framework.

Thompson, J., Wrye, T., Jenkins, M., and Campbell, C. 2018. "Accessibility at the Enterprise Level: Searching for a Cohesive Voice within a Fractured Ecosystem." *EDUCAUSE Review*, August 18. https://er.educause.edu/blogs/2018/8/accessibility-at-the-enterprise-level-searching-for-a-cohesive-voice-within-a-fractured-ecosystem.

Tobin, T. J. 2014. "Increase Online Student Retention with Universal Design for Learning." *Quarterly Review of Distance Education, 15*(3): 13–24. https://thomasjtobin.com/QRDE.UDL.Article.pdf.

Tobin, T. J. 2018. "Re-framing UDL for Broader Adoption in Higher Education: UDL and Mobile Learners." AHEAD Accessing Higher Ground presentation paper. https://www.dropbox.com/scl/fi/kfga2pq177tx01ag4zg11/20181114-AHEAD-Higher-Ground-Tobin-UDL-Jedi-White-Paper.pdf?rlkey=skpe6ftrp2x1gtd3i0gt3c3si&dl=0.

Tobin, T. J. 2024. *Syllabus: Universal Design for Learning Champions Seminar.* Moraine Park Technical College. https://www.dropbox.com/scl

/fi/v5on4q9v2bwxom8f5k20c/20240129-20240422-Moraine-Park-Technical-College-UDL-Champions-Seminar-Syllabus.pdf?rlkey=ulv678socdra9vl1cwb8biqll&dl=0

Tobin, T. J., and Behling, K. T. 2018. *Reach Everyone, Teach Everyone: Universal Design for Learning in Higher Education*. West Virginia University Press.

Trammell, J., and Hathaway, M. 2007. "Help-seeking Patterns in College Students with Disabilities." *Journal of Postsecondary Education and Disability, 20*(1): 4–15.

University of Cincinnati. 2020. *University of Cincinnati's Electronic Accessibility Policy*. https://www.uc.edu/content/dam/refresh/accessibility-62/eit-policy/EIT%20Accessibility%20Policy%204.5.2018.pdf.

University of Nebraska System. 2023. *NU Digital Accessibility Training*. teaching.unl.edu/workshops/digital-accessibility-series/.

University of Wisconsin–Madison. 2003. "Use of Facilities and Land. Policy UW-6000." *UW–Madison Policy Library*. https://policy.wisc.edu/library/UW-6000.

University of Wisconsin–Madison. 2019. *Strategic Framework 2020–2025*. https://strategicframework.wisc.edu/.

Webb, N. L. 1999. "Alignment of Science and Mathematics Standards and Assessments in Four States." *Research Monograph* 18. National Science Foundation. https://eric.ed.gov/?id=ED440852.

White, S. W., Ollendick, T. H., and Bray, B. C. 2011. "College Students on the Autism Spectrum: Prevalence and Associated Problems." *Autism, 15*(6): 683–701. https://doi.org/10.1177/1362361310393363.

World Wide Web Consortium. 2022. *WCAG 2 Overview*. https://www.w3.org/WAI/standards-guidelines/wcag/.

Wright, M. C. 2023. *Centers for Teaching and Learning: The New Landscape in Higher Education*. Johns Hopkins University Press.

Yan, J. 2023. "An empathetic look into an urgent need to rethink accessibility and inclusive design—Part 1." *Digication Scholars* podcast, *3*(28). Guest Marc Thompson. Posted June 14, 2023, by Digication. YouTube, 30:42. https://youtu.be/rjqKKoOI8Wo.

Zhang, L., Carter, R. A., Greene, J. A., and Bernacki, M. L. 2024. "Unraveling Challenges with the Implementation of Universal Design for Learning: A Systematic Literature Review." *Educational Psychology Review, 36*(35). https://doi.org/10.1007/s10648-024-09860-7.

Zhang, L., Carter, R. A., and Hoekstra, N. J. 2023. "A Critical Analysis of Universal Design for Learning in the U.S. Federal Education Law."

Policy Futures in Education, 22(4): 469–474. https://doi.org/10.1177/14782103231179530.

Zhu, M. 2021. "Limited Contracts, Limited Quality? Effects of Adjunct Instructors on Student Outcomes." *Economics of Education Review,* 85(1). https://doi.org/10.1016/j.econedurev.2021.102177.

INDEX

Page numbers of illustrations appear in *italic* type.

TEACHING, ENGAGING, AND THRIVING
IN HIGHER ED SERIES

James M. Lang and Michelle D. Miller, Series Editors

Other books in the series:

A Pedagogy of Kindness
Catherine J. Denial

A Teacher's Guide to Learning Student Names:
Why You Should, Why It's Hard, How You Can
Michelle D. Miller

The Present Professor:
Authenticity and Transformational Teaching
Elizabeth A. Norell

The Opposite of Cheating:
Teaching for Integrity in the Age of AI
Tricia Bertram Gallant and David A. Rettinger

Making Writing Meaningful:
A Guide for Higher Education
Michele Eodice, Anne Ellen Geller, and Neal Lerner

Snafu EDU:
Teaching and Learning When Things Go Wrong
in the College Classroom
Jessamyn Neuhaus

Empowered:
A Woman Faculty of Color's Guide to Teaching and Thriving
Chavella T. Pittman

The Joyful Online Teacher:
Finding Our Fizz in Asynchronous Classes
Flower Darby

www.ingramcontent.com/pod-product-compliance
Lightning Source LLC
LaVergne TN
LVHW100921110826
845155LV00035B/39

9780806197067